W9-CNX-867

MANAGING PUBLIC LANDS

in the PUBLIC INTEREST

ENVIRONMENTAL REGENERATION SERIES

Edited by
William R. Eblen
Ruth A. Eblen

Other Volumes in the Series

John Cairns, Jr. and Ruth Patrick, Editors:
MANAGING WATER RESOURCES, 1986

MANAGING PUBLIC LANDS

in the PUBLIC INTEREST

EDITED BY
BENJAMIN C. DYSART III
AND
MARION CLAWSON

ENVIRONMENTAL
REGENERATION SERIES

PRAEGER

New York
Westport, Connecticut
London

Library of Congress Cataloging-in-Publication Data

Managing public lands in the public interest.

(Environmental regeneration series)
Bibliography: p.
Includes index.
1. Public lands—Management.   2. Public interest.
3. Nature conservation.   I. Dysart, Benjamin C.
II. Clawson, Marion, 1905–   .   III. Series.
HD156.M329   1988   333.1   87–38117
ISBN 0–275–92990–6 (alk. paper)

Library of Congress Catalog Card Number: 87–38117

ISBN: 0–275–92990–6

First published in 1988

Praeger Publishers, One Madison Avenue, New York, NY 10010
A division of Greenwood Press, Inc.

Printed in the United States of America

The paper used in this book complies with the
Permanent Paper Standard issued by the National
Information Standards Organization (Z39.48–1984).

10   9   8   7   6   5   4   3   2   1

CONTENTS

SERIES PREFACE

> Now and then in my dreams, I see a place where one might initiate
> and publicize programs to give the environment movement a po-
> sitive constructive philosophy that would complement the present
> defensive attitude of environmental conservation and protection.
> (René Dubos 1975)

The René Dubos Center for Human Environments, a nonprofit education and research organization, was founded by the eminent scientist/
humanist in 1975 to focus on the humanistic and social aspects of
environmental problems. Whereas other organizations deal with the
protection of the environment, the Dubos Center is primarily concerned
with the interplay between human life and environmental situations.
It complements the defensive policies of the environmental movement
by emphasizing the creative aspects of human interventions into nature.

In 1981, Dr. Dubos convened an international conference to honor
Lady Jackson, Barbara Ward, who died in May of 1981—for it was their
plan to commemorate the 10th anniversary of the historic United Nations Conference on the Human Environment held in Stockholm in
1972. I had agreed, along with some 30 world leaders, to help him carry
out their plan to assess the progress made in the first decade with a
view to developing an action agenda for a more hopeful and positive
future. It had been my great privilege, as Secretary-General of the Stockholm Conference, to introduce René Dubos and Barbara Ward and to
enlist their cooperation in producing, with the support of some 100
other leaders from around the world, the book *Only One Earth*, which
became the principal source of guidance and inspiration for that conference.

René Dubos died on February 20, 1982, his 81st birthday. Mrs. Dubos, his colleagues, and the conveners all agreed that the convocation, although it had to be delayed, should go on as a living memorial to René Dubos as well as to Barbara Ward—and as a means of ensuring that the work and mission of René Dubos would continue through the Center that he founded, which bears his name and which continues his work.

I was honored to be invited to serve as Chairman of The International Convocation for World Environmental Regeneration that took place in February 1983, at the Waldorf-Astoria in New York City.

On the last day of the conference, a special meeting was held at The Rockefeller University to develop the action agenda for the Dubos Center's forum program. It calls for constructive dialogue among diverse authorities with an emphasis on sharing strategies that have proven to be significant in dealing with specific issues within each of the following areas addressed at the International Convocation:

• Environment and Human Health
• Managing Water Resources
• Land and Human Settlements
• Science, Technology and Human Values.

The practical purpose of The René Dubos Center's forum program is to acquire and integrate knowledge needed by the general public, not technical but rather focused on costs, benefits, and long-range consequences of the issues, to help formulate policies for the resolution of environmental conflicts and for the creation of new environmental values.

The workshops at each forum emphasize constructive dialogue and evaluation of major issues and the definition of areas of agreement and disagreement among the participating authorities who create, enforce, and are affected by environmental legislation. Case histories of creative solutions are cited whenever possible.

One tangible product of the Dubos Forum Program is this series of Environmental Regeneration books. The first book on *Managing Water Resources*, edited by John Cairns, Jr., and Ruth Patrick, was based on the Dubos Forum of the same name. *Managing Public Lands in the Public Interest* is the first of two volumes generated by the Dubos Forum on land management and edited by Benjamin C. Dysart III and Marion Clawson. It is hoped that the process begun at each forum will be continued and enhanced by publishing the findings and opinions of scientists and policymakers from all sectors of our society. In this way, the ripple effect of these dialogues begun among a small group of authorities will suggest creative new solutions to the environmental problems facing the human community.

Maurice F. Strong

ACKNOWLEDGMENTS

We are indebted to Dr. Dysart's secretary, Miss Patsy A. Phillips, for her assistance in the many organizational and editorial duties rendered during the preparation of this volume for publication. We also wish to thank her for typing and retyping several complete drafts of the book. Her good humor, persistence, and pleasant demeanor were tried on a few occasions in dealing with the editors and the other contributors; but her great professionalism regularly prevailed to the benefit of our product.

We would also like to thank Ada Louise Steirer for doing an excellent job in compiling the index for this book.

MANAGING PUBLIC LANDS

in the PUBLIC INTEREST

1

MANAGING PUBLIC LANDS IN THE PUBLIC INTEREST: AN OVERVIEW

Marion Clawson and Benjamin C. Dysart III

ABSTRACT

Historically, the public ownership of land has been an integral part of American society, culture, economy, and political structure. This was true both in the colonial period and throughout the nineteenth century, as settlement moved across the continent, fueled in part by the ready availability of public lands for private use. Beginning in the late nineteenth century—and continuing with increased force in this century— there has been a marked determination to retain in public ownership very large acreages of land, to be held, managed, and used for many purposes.

Key Words: public lands, public interest, private use, federal agencies, multiple use, resource management, public policy

NATURE OF PUBLIC LANDS

When "public lands" are mentioned, most people immediately think of federally owned lands. These are indeed extensive in area, including about one-third of the total land area of the United States. They include the national park system, national forests, extensive areas managed by the Bureau of Land Management, federal wildlife refuges, military reservations, and many other types of federal ownership. There is some federal land in every state, although the largest acreages are in the west, where in some states they amount to more than half of the total land area.

But it is a mistake to overlook the substantial areas of land owned by the states for parks, natural and wilderness areas, forests, wildlife areas, and as remnants of school and other grant lands. In some states these acreages are substantial in comparison with the total land area.

It is equally a mistake to overlook the land owned by cities, counties, and other units of local government for schools, parks, and forests, and of course for many kinds of public buildings. While these areas are small in relation to the larger areas of state and federal land, these locally owned public areas are often highly important to and intensively used by many segments of the public.

The largest areas of publicly owned land are used for forestry, recreation, and grazing, as well as for mineral production, and are predominantly rural. But there are significant areas of publicly owned land that are located within cities. While the acreages of publicly-owned urban land are small, their economic and social value is very high.

USE OF PUBLIC LANDS

Publicly owned lands are usually used by private persons for many different purposes. The forest products company harvests timber, the rancher uses grazing land for his livestock, individuals visit the parks and fish and hunt in national forests, and so on. The only real exception to the private use of public lands is the use by the armed forces of military reservations. This private use of publicly owned land is as true for state and local government land as it is for federally owned land.

The relation between public ownership and private use creates problems for public land management but, at the same time, provides the opportunities for effective and productive management. The demands of the public may be as important as the ecological characteristics of the land. If there was no public interest in using the national forests for outdoor recreation, for example, the management of these lands could be very different. The same is true for other uses of public land— it is the demands of the public that provide both opportunities and problems for land managers.

Demands by individuals for the use of public lands are not always benign. In recent years, illegal use of national forests to grow marijuana has become a serious problem. This illegal use not only threatens the safety of the U.S. Forest Service employees but deprives the rest of the public of use of the lands in question. While this is perhaps the most flagrant example, trespass on public lands by persons for unauthorized and harmful purposes is unfortunately not uncommon.

USERS OF PUBLIC LANDS

The users of public lands are varied, though they may not be a totally representative cross-section of the whole American populace. Some income classes have little opportunity to use public lands; nevertheless the users of public lands are almost as diverse as the general population.

Different users of public land naturally enough tend to look at the land from different perspectives. The wilderness lover sees a wonderful stand of virgin old-growth timber while the lumberman or forester sees the same trees as being ripe for harvest or even overmature. The hunter sees a prime wildlife habitat supporting a healthy deer population where a nice buck might be harvested, while the animal lover sees a protected refuge for the deer. Each sees and appraises the natural resource in terms of his or her personal knowledge, experiences, background, values, and interests.

Out of these divergent perceptions, differing ideas arise as to what is "right," "reasonable," "proper," "responsible," "fair," "equitable," or "efficient" in the management of the lands and their renewable and nonrenewable resources. Distinct ideas of what "multiple use" really means—or should mean—also develop in practice. Differences occur over which uses are desirable, which are compatible, which must be subordinated to others, and which must be excluded altogether. While such questions have scientific resource management components, they are basically questions about people's values, goals, aspirations, biases, fears, and priorities rather than about resources per se.

NATURE OF THIS BOOK

This book is a collection of essays on the management of public lands. The essays were written by distinguished persons with very different backgrounds and interests. Each was asked to write on an aspect of public land management, following a somewhat standard format. The contributors were allowed to develop their essays in the manner they thought most suitable. The editors of this volume participated as members of the Dubos Land Use Forum Steering Committee in selecting the topics and the authors. They also made suggestions to the authors for the revision of first drafts; but the essays included here are those which contributors submitted for final publication.

The result of this process is a book less tightly structured than if it had been written by a single author. For the same reason, it is a book which is richer in details and in perspectives on the problems of public land management.

COMMON ELEMENTS

While the essays reflect the varied interests and experiences of the authors, the editors believe there are a number of elements common to all the essays. These are the following:

1. Public ownership of land in the United States is here to stay. Some areas might be sold for private purposes and other areas of land now privately owned may be purchased by some unit of government. But total or majority disposal of public lands—federal, state, and local—is simply unthinkable.

2. Private use of public lands must continue; these lands are owned for their public use values and not for the satisfaction of their managers alone. This does not imply that private use should not be limited in some cases to a carrying capacity of the site, nor does it imply that every kind of use should be made on every area. Quite to the contrary. Private use of public areas typically has to be constrained by scientifically sound management rules, both to protect the integrity and long-term productivity of the area and to avoid undue interference with other legitimate users.

3. Multiple use of public lands is not only highly desirable but, to a degree, unavoidable. Different persons have different concepts of what constitutes proper multiple use, and difficult problems often arise in deciding this in practice. But consideration of all possible uses, and conscious, well-informed choice of that mixture of uses which seems most productive for a type of public land or for an individual specific site, is necessary to satisfy public needs. This is a difficult challenge, but the public has a right to expect the best and most professional management of its lands.

4. Sound public policy requires the preservation of the basic productive capacity of our public lands. This does not necessarily preclude sport hunting, timber harvest, or even some short-term degradation of sites, such as a camp-ground. But it does require that the basic productive capacity such as timber growth or wildlife habitat be maintained for the long term.

5. Planning for use in the management of public lands is not only necessary but also unavoidable. Every action in the present depends for its rationale on some concept of the future. There is substantial dissatisfaction today with the planning practice of public land-managing agencies, but the solution lies in better planning, not in an effort to avoid all planning.

6. The public must be adequately and properly involved in the planning for use of all kinds of publicly owned lands and associated resources. There are obvious problems and limitations to public involvement, and there are lots of ways to do it poorly but there is no viable alternative to public involvement. Successful managers of public lands consistently find that public involvement—when done well and in good faith—produces better plans that receive and deserve more public confidence and that better serve the public interest.

2

OBSTRUCTIONISM RECONSIDERED, OR IN DEFENSE OF NIMBY AND LULU

David Charles Masselli

ABSTRACT

Bitter and emotional disputes over the siting of large facilities have given rise to calls for "streamlined" or "rationalized" siting laws and procedures. Generally such calls are made by proponents of building the facilities. This chapter examines failures in the current system which arise from its inherent tendency to approve all proposed projects, rather than to quickly terminate many proposals.

Key Words: obstructionism, facility site planning, siting process, environmental impact statement, National Environmental Policy Act, public participation, NIMBY, Clean Air Act, RCRA, decision making

INTRODUCTION

Discussions of the problems associated with major facility siting tend to focus on purported inefficiencies with the siting process as it exists in many regions of the country.[1] The "siting process," we are told, is too protracted, too uncertain, too expensive, too subject to emotionalism. Because of these flaws in the system, it is becoming almost impossible to site or build major facilities. This had led to repeated calls for a rationalized and streamlined decision-making process for siting.

Such calls are almost always made by those seeking to build projects, rather than those opposing them. Their proposals would limit the ability of project opponents to challenge or delay the issuance of permits once they had been approved by administrative bodies and would occasionally force permit issuers to act within specified time frames.

A cottage industry has grown of professional siting reformers. At a moment's notice, they will appear at a legislative hearing reciting tales of "horrible occurrences" during which rational and reasonable siting proposals were hung up by procedural delays and tortured by irrational forces opposing process and development.[2] Often the same stories are recycled again and again, sometimes in versions that bear as much resemblance to what really took place as Ronald Reagan's tales of the welfare queen bore to the realities of AFDC. Later, slightly sanitized versions of these performances will appear in such unbiased journals as the *Rocky Mountain Law Review*.

As one who has, for most of the past decade, represented parties vigorously opposed to the siting of various large—and I might add, rather unpleasant—facilities in their backyards, I view much of what is written about the problems of siting in professional journals with a somewhat jaundiced eye. When has delay of a controversial major energy facility brought the slightest negative consequences to any but its promoters and those who stood to make money from it? The republic has yet to crumble because of the failure to site a transcontinental oil pipeline, a coal slurry pipeline, a natural gas pipeline across Alaska, an oil port in Maine, a molybdenum mine in Colorado, or floating nuclear power plants off the coast of New Jersey—to name just a few of the more celebrated subjects of siting clashes during the last decade.[3] (One suspects that the sponsors of several of the projects listed above awake each morning thanking their lucky stars that they did not have that success in reaching prompt siting decisions that brought the Washington Public Power Supply System to such a peak of glory.)

Furthermore, I am not at all impressed with that line of thought which holds that much of the opposition to facility siting comes from those basely motivated by the NIMBY ("not in my backyard") or LULU ("locally unacceptable land use") syndromes. The most eloquent NIMBY-bashers tend to be located in communities like Potomac, Maryland; Knoxville, Tennessee; Fairfield County, Connecticut; and other neighborhoods which for inexplicable reasons rarely seem to be the proposed sites for nuclear waste dumps, coal-fired power plants, or other such noxious facilities. I see nothing wrong with wanting to protect the quality of life—and even the property values—of one's community.

Despite the failure to pass legislation creating an Energy Mobilization Board to snip red tape for major energy projects, the country seems to have weathered the worst of the energy crisis. Many of the projects that were the subject of successful challenge suffered from obvious economic problems in addition to their environmental risks. From the vantage point of the present, it is relatively easy to question the wisdom of building unneeded oil refineries in environmentally sensitive harbors or bludgeoning national parks in Utah to supply the glutted California electricity market with coal. Undoubtedly, such economic uncertainties make a project ripest for successful opposition at the same time that precarious profit projections make it most difficult for project proponents to acquiesce in expensive mitigation.

Does this mean that the current facility siting process is acceptable? Far from it. It is a disaster. Many of the charges made by those who would like to see faster siting decisions are true. The process can be interminable. Politics and emotionalism can intrude on decision making. It may be virtually impossible to site certain types of facilities. But this is only part of the problem, the part most apparent to the proponents of siting of facilities. If anything, the problem with the process is that it allows too many projects that should not be built at all to get through; and it fails to make obvious and rational changes in many others that ought to be built, but not along the exact blueprints of their proponents.

THE VIEW FROM THE OTHER SIDE

There is another side to the facility siting dilemma. For those who face the potential impacts of major industrial facilities, the siting process as it exists in most regions of this country provides them with almost no opportunity to protect their legitimate interests. It is expensive to invoke the process. Debate over many of the most important real issues is often excluded. And the outcome is rigged: No application to site a major facility is ever turned down.

If your immediate reaction to this last statement is to consider it a wild exaggeration or a bit of florid rhetoric, consider the answers to the following questions:

—How many applications to construct a nuclear power plant have been denied by the Nuclear Regulatory Commission (NRC)?

—How many environmental impact statements (EIS) for major facilities have been issued with a preferred alternative that the project not be built?

—How many western coal-fired power plants have been denied prevention of significant deterioration (PSD) permits?

As you might suspect, the number of instances of any of the above occurrences can be counted on the thumbs of one hand. The NRC has turned down one nuclear power plant application, and the EIS for the Tellico Dam recommended it not be built (the project was built anyway). When western coal-fired plants appear to violate the Class–1 PSD limitations of the Clean Air Act designed to protect national parks, the U.S. Environmental Protection Agency (EPA) invariably approves new modeling procedures which show the pollution dissipating just short of park boundaries.[4]

Had siting merely been a matter of collecting approval for the requisite permits, the SOHIO pipeline, the ETSI coal slurry pipeline, the Mount Emmons moly mine, the Machiasport oil terminal, the Hampshire synfuels plant, the Kaiparowits power plants, and a host of other facilities would be up and running. Nor can their demise be attributed to delays in the administrative aspects of the siting process. Indeed, most of these proposals were rubber-stamped with some alacrity by the various boards and agencies with siting responsibility. They met their Waterloo in the courts and the stock market.

The dirty little secret of our siting laws is they are not designed to say "no".[5]

So, if you awake one morning and discover that a corporate or governmental entity has taken it into its head to build something god-awful in your backyard, you know that you are in for a struggle. First, the chances of any administrative or appointed body turning the proposal down are reasonably close to zero, even if the proposal is totally off the wall. Second, there is a high probability that what bothers you about the facility might not even be considered legally relevant to whatever deliberations take place. Third, you will probably have to go out and hire both technical experts and a legal staff. Fourth, you know that you will eventually end up in court; and if by some chance you win at the first level, you will have to fight an appeal.

Your opponent will be well financed, sometimes with its own resources and sometimes from the public trough, either directly, as in the case of a unit of government seeking to build a facility, or indirectly, as in the case of your local public utility. Also, it is quite likely that the siting proponent has been formulating its plans for a long time, has already assembled its experts, paid for its studies, and is ready to proceed. You may be forced to cover the same ground in several weeks or months that the proponent has had years to examine. And after the proposal is announced, in its most favorable light, it may take you months or years to dig through all of the fine print and understand what is actually being proposed. Sometimes you will face a moving target of conceptual plans, preliminary engineering designs, and proposed—but changeable—process units.

SITING: THE BATTLE BEHIND THE BATTLE

Notwithstanding these facts, many people feel strongly enough about their backyards, so siting challenges are rather frequent, notwithstanding the costs. And while NIMBY may be a sign of excess emotionalism, the participants in siting struggles are generally hardheaded enough to realize that they will not achieve their aim by convincing an administrative law judge that planned discharges (from a facility that exists only on paper) will exceed a federal limit by two millimicrons or what-ever.[6] They will prevail by either (1) making the struggle too costly—in terms of delay or excess costs mandated by siting decision makers—to the proponents of the project or (2) by convincing elected officials with some authority over the decision that their political futures may be adversely affected by allowing it to be built.

This sets the stage for siege warfare. And depending upon the terrain, the challengers may stand a reasonable chance of success. There is a deep irony in the key to that success: because siting laws contain few objective standards for when projects should be rejected or seriously modified, they, of necessity, contain similarly few clearcut standards for when they should be approved.

In this respect, it might be useful to contrast siting laws with what might be called the "noncorrupt" model of zoning in many large cities. Zoning codes are, if anything, too replete with quantifiable detail. Everything from the height of a structure to the depth of a setback to the width and composition of interior walls may be spelled out for each zoning category. When an application is put forward, it is a relatively simple task to determine whether or not it complies with the require-ments. Residents in every area are on notice of what is possible and probable in the way of neighbors. Builders and developers know what steps they need to take to guarantee approval.

Of course an approach that might work in determining how any one of 10,000 tract houses should be constructed in a suburban county may be of little relevance in helping to site the one high-level waste repo-sitory in the county. (Its relevance to power plants, jails, solid waste disposal sites, and other facilities built by the gross is greater; but despite repeated calls for standardization in the abstract, project de-velopers tend to shun that approach in practice.) Conceptually, how-ever, this approach to land-use management stands at one end of a continuum. Most siting laws are spread across that continuum.

THE SITING CONTINUUM

Just how wide that continuum is might be seen by examining briefly the siting process as applied to the Union Oil Company's 10,000-barrel-per-day synfuels plant in western Colorado. One might imagine that such a project would have been subject to a raft of complex and lengthy siting proceedings, but in fact, the opposite was the case. The project was not built on federal lands, nor did it require a federal right-of-way, it did not affect any interstate waters, nor did it receive any of the traditional forms of federal funding. So no federal EIS was prepared. The state of Colorado has no state NEPA (National Environmental Pol-icy Act) law. While a PSD analysis was prepared, it was not required to examine the potential toxic emissions, of great concern from such a plant because they are currently unregulated under the Clean Air Act. Neither the state of Colorado nor the county in which the project was located had any facility siting legislation, so there were no required administrative hearings on the project. Local zoning and land-use planning ordinances were also relatively inapplicable. Thus, a billion-dollar facility using a relatively untried technology with potential environmental and health hazards was sited with almost no administrative or judicial oversight and relatively few public hearings.[7]

In discussing siting laws, it is important to remember that the siting process will vary depending upon: (1) the type of facility being sited, (2) the state in which it is being sited, (3) the ownership of land used for the site or rights-of-way, and (4) special circumstances—such as the presence of endangered species, impact of the project on wetlands or protected rivers, and proximity to parks or wilderness areas. It is almost impossible to develop a comprehensive taxonomy for the siting process, but for purposes of this discussion, I would like to look at the following six categories.

A TAXONOMY OF SITING PROCEDURES

Minimum Federal, Minimum State

This first category applies where a state had no special laws regarding this kind of facility and federal review was limited to a PSD review and a Section 404 dredge-and-fill review with no EIS. A hard-rock mine, a coal-fired power plant with no federal rights-of-ways, and a chemical facility in an eastern state might all be examples of this category.

Moderate Federal, Minimum State

This second category applies wherever NEPA requires a federal EIS or other site-specific federal law is operative and there is minimum state regulation. Examples of this category are large industrial facilities in many western states which require rights-of-ways across federal lands, large coal mines, and certain kinds of solid waste disposal facilities.

Moderate Federal, Moderate State

This third category would apply where a state has laws governing the construction of this kind of facility that go beyond mere state administration of delegated authority under such laws as the Clean Air, Clean Water, and Resource Conservation and Recovery Act (RCRA) laws (either more restrictive provisions under these laws or facility-specific legislation).

Special Circumstances Federal

This fourth category covers situations where the application of such specific federal laws as the Endangered Species Act, Wild and Scenic Rivers Act, Executive Orders 11988 and 11990 (relating to flood plain management and the protection of wetlands), or the National Historic Preservation Act can have a significant impact on whether a facility can be placed in a specific location. The Class-I siting limitations under the Clean Air Act have a similar impact. These laws are generally designed to protect a certain place rather than regulate a specific kind of facility.

Comprehensive State Siting Laws

This fifth category covers those states that have industrial siting laws which give the state the right to disapprove or place conditions on the siting of a facility even after all other permit conditions have been met. The primary examples of this kind of law are the Montana, Wyoming, and North Dakota siting laws. It is important to differentiate this kind of law from those state laws or administrative procedures which merely provide for a consolidation or coordination of permitting, but do not add any additional requirements or provide for discretion in setting conditions. (North Dakota, for example, has both: The Public Service Commission must grant a siting certificate, and the Department of Health handles virtually all permits.)

I do not consider traditional power plant certificate-of-need proceedings to fall into this category. In practice, these are generally analyses of whether a facility might provide useful power, not whether a given facility is the best alternative, and certainly not whether or not all of the other elements of the facility—such as its physical location, construction and operation plans, impact on the local community, etc.— are appropriate.

The discretionary nature of the siting decision makes this approach the most susceptible to political and economic pressures. Thus, western states that were driving hard bargains in the late 1970s took a very different tack in the recent energy bust. This is not as craven as it may seem: Some elements of laxity may have been justified by the fact that there was far less development going on than had been hoped (or feared) and that different calculations of advantage may reasonably be drawn in markedly changed circumstances.

Federal Preemption

This sixth situation applies where federal law preempts the application of inconsistent state or local regulation. Federal preemption is strongest in areas involving the construction of nuclear power plants and the siting of nuclear facilities. However, elements of federal preemption may be found in areas such as the development of federally leased minerals (*Ventura County vs. Gulf Oil*, 601 F. 2d, 1080, 9th Civ. 1979), offshore oil (*Secretary of the Interior vs. California*, 464 U.S. 312, 1984), and oil and gas pipeline construction. It is noteworthy that many of the industries that most strongly advocate a strong state role in setting air and water quality standards—where economic competition could lead to competition to lower environmental costs—strongly support federal preemption for siting facilities which are generally unpopular, like nuclear and toxic waste dumps.

What about NEPA?

By now I am certain that a good many readers of this chapter are sitting on the edge of their chairs saying "Why isn't this guy talking about NEPA and its role in the siting process? Surely it cures most of what he is complaining about?" Well, NEPA does play an important role in some siting disputes, but not nearly the role many people think.[8]

First, despite appearances to the contrary, NEPA is not omnipresent.[9] Environmental impact statements are only required when a federal agency wishes to take a "major federal action significantly affecting the environment." Thus, many purely state actions, such as the siting of prisons or toxic waste dumps, are unaffected. And some federal actions which certainly appear to be major are exempted from NEPA: These include almost all permitting decisions under the Clean Air Act and many permits under the Clean Water Act.

Second, NEPA is purely procedural. It imposes no requirements on any project, other than that it be examined, along with some reasonable alternatives, to determine environmental impact. Even should that analysis disclose tremendous environmental or social damage associated with the project, NEPA places no requirement on the federal decision maker other than that it make "a fully informed and well considered decision" (*Vermont Yankee Nuclear Power Plant vs. Natural Resources Defense Council*, 435 U.S. 519, 1978). Once the federal agency has jumped through the procedural hoops, it is free to approve just about anything it wishes.

To the project developer, NEPA is an unavoidable delay, though oftentimes one of relatively short duration. To the federal agency, NEPA imposes an exercise in discipline during which the patina of rational thought glosses written declarations (that is, the Record of Decision) after which the agency is free to return to its normal modes of comprehension. To the committed NIMBYite, NEPA may be a snare and delusion. I am continually amazed at the number of people I deal with who are sure that NEPA will stop a project, that something in the law makes agencies do the right thing, and that NEPA lawsuits can be successfully brought to overturn failures in judgment. The only failure in judgment which is probably punishable is the failure to do an EIS at all, a lapse in judgment which is declining, though not totally out of fashion.

So, is NEPA irrelevant in siting struggles? Hardly. There are three reasons why NEPA is so important in fights over energy development. First, it is a stop sign: Nothing final can happen until its compliances have been met. Second, it is an information process: NEPA, properly used, lays bare enormous amounts of information about a proposed project. This information may not only have a bearing on the particular decision being made by the federal agency preparing an environmental impact statement, but also may affect many other decision makers, including political and financial interests who make decisions that are not constrained by regulation. And last, NEPA is cheap and easy to use. Anyone who can speak or write can participate since the legal procedures are relatively simple.[10]

Where it applies, NEPA prevents project opponents from being steam-rolled. It gives them time to organize, helps them find the necessary information needed to make their case, and often provides a public forum in which to develop opposition. It is often a necessary precondition to success, but it is not dispositive.

The Missing Elements

A striking phenomenon in many siting struggles is the prevalence of missing elements in the siting process. By "missing elements," I mean those potentially harmful or otherwise undesirable attributes of a facility that are not addressed in the siting process as applied to that facility. Like the voice of the Commendatore in Don Giovanni, they are never onstage, but always present.

Let me draw two examples from the moribund synthetic fuels industry to demonstrate how the siting process is often riddled with missing elements. Were I faced with a coal-based synthetic fuels plant as a neighbor, I would be most concerned with two potential health hazards. The first would be the presence of various aromatic hydrocarbons with carcinogenic potential as fugitive emissions from the facility. The second would be the possible leaching of wastewater sludges and other chemicals from the solid waste disposal facility associated with the plant.[11]

Worried about these risks, I might prepare to address them in a siting hearing of some sort. After all, even in our Minimum Federal, Minimum State scenario, the plant will be subject to a relatively rigorous PSD air quality review with a public hearing. Furthermore, regardless of whether the solid waste from the plant is stored on-site or shipped off-site, its eventual disposal will be subject to regulation under Part C of RCRA. Unfortunately, I will be sorely disappointed in my efforts to raise these issues or to use the siting process to seek mitigating methods.

Under the Clean Air Act, no standards of performance were ever developed for synthetic fuels plants, nor were the suspect hydrocarbons ever listed as hazardous air pollutants subject to Section 111. The PSD review focuses on the so-called "criteria pollutants," with specific numerical limitations set only for sulfur dioxide and particulates. Tucked away in the interstices of the PSD review process are requirements that process design information be given on the emission of any "regulated pollutants" which has been interpreted to include not only criteria and hazardous pollutants but also other pollutants regulated in any new-source performance standard. This adds emissions of such substances as fluorides, sulfuric acid mists, hydrogen sulfide, and other sulfur compounds to the list which must be studied and are subject to best available control technology (BACT). Some of the substances of concern may fall into this group, depending on the technology used; others will not. Even for those that do, no standards or criteria for what is acceptable exist.

Concerns about leachates from synfuels waste piles will fall on more deaf ears. Although there is general agreement that this may be the most significant environmental impact associated with the operation of synfuels facilities, a little-noticed provision of law defines these wastes as being "nonhazardous" pursuant to RCRA. This does not mean that Congress, by fiat, was able to guarantee that such wastes will not bring harm, merely that it was able to decide that such wastes will not be regulated, regardless of their potential to bring harm.

Thus, in this hypothetical, two risks which are generally acknowledged to exist and to be serious will not be addressed in the siting process. This will not make the potential for harm go away. Nor will it defuse opposition that is based on these risks. Instead, it often means that other issues—which can be addressed in the siting process—will become proxies for the missing or excluded elements.[12]

There are serious and obvious problems with this approach. In addition to the inefficiency of arguing over proxies when the real issues are left off the table, the use of proxies virtually precludes compromise. If you cannot raise the issue of toxic emissions, but can raise the issue of impacts on visibility in a distant park, you may very well do so. Unfortunately, almost every solution proposed to the proxy problem will have little effect on the "real" problem. So the chances of compromise—or conflict resolution—are minimal.

If this problem were limited to a dying industry such as synfuels, it would have only academic interest. However, my own experience convinces me that the problem is widespread. There is a serious disjunction between what is regulated and what is feared. Like Topsy, our scheme of environmental regulation just grew. We regulated garden-variety air pollutants to the teeth, but not toxic emissions which can kill. We regulate sporadic impacts rigorously, while ignoring the day-to-day impacts that are most grating. Most importantly, we regulate effects on health, but not on other critical factors associated with the quality of life.

Does this mean that we should not regulate conventional air pollutants or health impacts? No. There is an important and legitimate public purpose in most of the existing regulations on the books. But we should not be surprised when facilities which seem to pass the legislative criteria are subject to vigorous attack and opposition. Nor should we denigrate that attack as being mere emotionalism.

It is impossible to list all of the missing factors in siting procedures. Some will be present in certain states or for certain facilities and not for others, but among those which are most often missing are: (1) impact on the local community lifestyle, (2) possibility of a disastrous outcome, (3) effect on property values, (4) impacts of construction—rather than operation—of the facility, and (5) effect of the boom-and-bust cycle associated with most projects.

Not surprisingly, many of these concerns are far removed from the normal subjects of "environmental" regulation. Their absence is felt most acutely in situations where there is minimal federal and state regulation and, at the other end of the spectrum, where there is federal preemption. The ability to raise these issues—or almost any other issues—to analyze them and to force mitigation on the project proponent is greatest where discretionary state siting laws exist.

In this procedure there is no "checklist" of permits, where the project proponent examines the relevant laws and knows exactly what must be done to obtain each and every permit. It will not "streamline" facility siting as that term is normally understood. But it may lessen some elements of the gridlock that now afflicts certain types of facility siting.

It may be argued that the uncertainty associated with the state siting law approach is in direct contrast to the "zoning" model earlier espoused as a paradigm of certainty and promptness. In the abstract this is true. But zoning laws did not spring to life full-blown. They were a reflection of experience and of a political consensus about what kinds of impacts were acceptable and where. There is no reason that comprehensive siting laws cannot also be developed in a way that adds certain specificity to their application. That this requires making political judgments about costs and benefits should be no barrier; those judgments will be made implicitly if not made explicitly.

Finally, it should be pointed out that the nature of local government in this country is such that it is very difficult for one group of people to decide that it is acceptable to site unpleasant facilities in another's backyard, unless the sitees agree and, normally, unless they receive some kind of benefit in return for serving the greater public good.

One problem with most cost-benefit analyses—such as those performed for siting waste dumps and jails—is that they focus on the macro side (of course society needs dumps and jails) while ignoring the micro side (the most severely affected residents are facing a distinct and tangible cost and reaping only the vaguest benefit).

Other forms of compensation, such as the bringing of jobs and economic improvement to a community, are equally capricious. Farmers and ranchers I have represented in controversies over the siting of coal mines in the northern Plains states often find this a "heads I lose, tails you win" proposition. Before energy-related development, they had jobs and a certain life-style. The new facility destroys much of the life-style, may directly impact the viability of their current businesses, and the new prosperity often has the impact of driving up the costs they must pay for goods, labor, and local services. What may be a great deal to the builders of trailer parks and the manufacturers of D9 dozers is a financial disaster to them. Unfortunately, the streams of costs and benefits from such projects are rarely congruent.

TOWARD AN HONEST SITING PROCEDURE

I have no magic answer for the current siting dilemma. But I would suggest that so long as critical aspects of the siting decision are not directly on the table for modification or rejection and so long as there is no method of compensating those being asked to bear costs associated with the attainment of benefits for the greater community—however defined—the inclination of those imposed on by potential siting decisions will be to throw the kitchen sink into the process.

Those who argue for rationalization and streamlining must recognize that, fairly applied, they can be a two-edged sword. Rationalization implies that all impacts of a project be subject to review—not just some arbitrarily determined subset—and that objective standards be developed to specify what must be demonstrated by opponents of a facility to cause denial of a permit or modification of a proposal. Furthermore, any streamlining of the process at the back end would seem to require some streamlining at the beginning, including de novo rejection of some proposals without the need for expensive citizen opposition.

Finally, a rationalized siting process requires that public input not be totally divorced from public influence. A myriad of hearings, briefings, meetings, and other forms of interaction are of little value if the end product of the process never differs from the initial proposal.

In the absence of changes of this sort, we will continue to have siting by indirection. Facilities that disrupt the lives of communities and individuals will be attacked because of their potential impact on rare flora or fauna or the opacity of smoke plumes 100 miles away. Computer-generated environmental impact statements containing mendacious risk assessment which would do the Tobacco Institute proud will be attacked, not for their underlying falsity (judges wouldn't understand and the other side can probably buy more experts) but for failure to meet procedural niceties that many thought had disappeared after *Jaryndice vs. Jaryndice*. And, because virtue certainly does not reside on any one side, delaying and defensive procedures which might in one case save an area of great scenic beauty or protect a community from socioeconomic ruin can be just as easily used to prevent the construction of a sorely needed public facility.

The end result will be that some facilities that should be built might not, and many facilities will be built with a greater detrimental impact than is necessary.

NOTES

1. I use the term "siting process" to refer to all steps necessary in procuring the necessary permits to construct an industrial facility. The siting process can be further divided into three phases: the administrative, executive, and judicial. The administrative phase involves decision making by appointed officials pursuant to previously promulgated laws and regulations. The executive phase refers to discretionary decision making by elected officials. The judicial phase involves challenges to administrative and executive decision making on the grounds that the decision maker erred. In general, judicial challenges to decision making can be divided into two types: (1) allegations that the decision maker did not follow an applicable law and (2) allegations that the decision maker acted in an arbitrary or capricious manner in making a decision that was committed to his or her discretion.

2. The high point of organized "kvetching" over siting undoubtedly occurred during the consideration of S. 1308, the Priority Energy Project Act of 1980 which would have created a federal Energy Mobilization Board (EMB) with the power to override and waive federal and state environmental laws to expedite non-nuclear energy projects. See U.S. Congress, Senate, S. Rep. No. 331, 96th Cong., 1st sess., 1979. A document prepared for the Senate Energy Committee lists 39 major projects that had been canceled or abandoned after

substantial expenditures due to "litigation and regulatory delays." See Van Ness, Feldman, and Sutcliffe, "Major Non-nuclear Energy Facility Project Terminations, Cancellations or Abandonments," Congressional Hearing Report 96–75, Part 2, 1979. Congress eventually rejected the EMB proposal.

In recent years, the pendulum has swung slightly in the opposite direction, with some studies casting doubt on the role that siting laws or abuses of the siting laws have played in the demise of these many projects. See Duerkson et al., *Siting New Industry: An Environmental Perspective* (Washington, D.C.: The Conservation Foundation, 1982). Skepticism about the "siting is death" thesis appeared to have characterized the views of the majority of the participants in the Dubos forum workshop at which this chapter was originally presented, though that is not to say that the participants accepted the views set forth here.

3. For those wishing to keep score, the projects referred to above are: (1) the SOHIO PACTEX pipeline designed to go from Long Beach, California, to Midland, Texas; (2) the ETSI (Energy Transmissions Systems, Inc.) coal slurry pipeline which was designed to carry coal from the Powder River Basin of Wyoming to Arkansas; (3) the Alaska Natural Gas Pipeline authorized by P.L. 94–586, 90 State 2903, 15 U.S.C. 719 *et seq.* designed to carry natural gas from Prudhoe Bay, Alaska, to the West Coast and Midwest in the Lower 48; (4) the AMAX Fort Emmons molybdenum mine; and (5) a proposal by General Electric to allow licensing of floating nuclear power plants which were to be built at a special facility in Florida.

4. An example of this may be seen in the shifting evaluations of air quality in North Dakota performed by the Department of the Interior as it approved various energy development schemes. The three units of Theodore Roosevelt National Park (TRNP) have the misfortune to be located downwind from the lignite belt of central North Dakota. In 1982, Interior issued an "Air Quality Information Supplement to the Fort Union Coal Region Draft Environmental Impact Statement" in which it used new baseline data and an altered air quality modeling regime to show that the development associated with proposed leasing would not exceed the limit. Following this analysis, Interior found that the Class-I PSD increment "already has been consumed or nearly consumed." Two years later, DOI considered a proposal for a synfuels plant in the same region. Once again, a new model described as including "the use of nonguideline techniques" was unveiled which found yet more unconsumed increment. See U.S. Department of the Interior, *Draft Environmental Impact Statement: Dunn-Nakota Methanol Project*, January 1985, Appendix D.4, p. 31.

5. An exception to this general rule is found in the unintended consequences of laws such as the Endangered Species Act (ESA). This is one reason why siting struggles so often revolve around attempts to locate the regional equivalent of the snail darter. But one should note that, despite its place in folklore, the snail darter did not scuttle the building of the Tellico Dam; and the ESA, while providing gainful employment for hordes of biologists and grist for hundreds of horror stories, has proved similarly ineffective in providing a veto over a single project.

6. To be both fair and realistic, it is unlikely that the proponents of a project will unveil a plan that they think is either (1) prohibited by the clear letter of the applicable law or (2) likely to be strongly opposed by the ultimate decision

maker. Thus, siting laws clearly have a significant and beneficial impact in preventing some proposals from ever seeing the light of day. My earlier statement about the forgone conclusion of most siting exercise was not meant to imply that siting decision makers allowed facilities clearly in violation of the law (although a good argument could be made that the NRC has done so on several occasions), but rather that they never reject and rarely modify the unwise proposal, no matter how compelling the evidence. The motto in facility siting seems to be: "That which is not forbidden is to be enthusiastically permitted."

7. As one who has been involved in opposing the Union Oil facility over a long period of time, I think it important that that fact be acknowledged. Nor do I wish to leave the impression that the facility is particularly unsafe because of the siting process it underwent or that it was the subject of widespread local opposition (which it was not). Rather, the Union Oil situation is an example of the vagaries of the siting process. Because of its location, the nature of the environmental risks involved, the type of funding used, etc., the number of hearings, studies, and so on was far less than would have occurred for a facility of similar complexity and potential impact located in a different area. By the same token, a relatively straightforward and conventional project in a different area might find itself subject to dozens of permit hearings.

8. The National Environmental Policy Act, P.L. 91–190, 42 U.S.C. 4371 et seq. Regulations for implementing the procedural provisions of NEPA are promulgated by the Council on Environmental Quality (CEQ), 40 CFR Parts 1500–1508.

9. The number of environmental impact statements has steadily declined over the past seven years. Figures compiled by CEQ: 1,355 statements filed in 1978; 1,273 in 1979; 966 in 1980; 1,033 in 1981; 808 in 1982; 677 in 1983; and 577 in 1984. Council on Environmental Quality, Fifteenth Annual Report of the Council on Environmental Quality, Washington, 1985, Table A–69. A review of all CEQ annual reports issued during this period shows that between 139 and 157 NEPA lawsuits were filed annually during this period with injunctions granted for 17 to 21 each year.

10. Lash and King, eds., The Synfuels Manual (New York: Natural Resources Defense Council, 1983), p. 218.

11. A more complete discussion of the particulars of these potential hazards can be found in Lash and King, eds., The Synfuels Manual (New York: Natural Resources Defense Council, 1983), chap. 4.

12. An interesting variant on missing elements was pioneered by the Nuclear Regulatory Commission which took to holding expensive generic inquiries into important areas of controversy and then adopting the results of such exercises as inalterable and unchallengeable received fact in subsequent proceedings. This effectively precluded reexamination of these matters. The most famous of these exercises produced the "Rasmussen Report" (more properly, The Reactor Safety Study, WASH–1400) which detailed down through many orders of magnitude the improbability of any serious nuclear accident sequence. Until supplanted by a later NRC document, the Rasmussen report was gospel in nuclear licensing hearing even though obviously fatuous.

3

MULTIPLE-USE CONSIDERATIONS
Marion Clawson

ABSTRACT

Although all land provides more than one kind of output or use, planned multiple use to attain a desired combination of outputs requires careful analysis for both public and private lands. Proposed multiple-use programs must be considered in terms of their physical and biological feasibility and consequences, economic efficiency, economic equity, conformity to dominant cultural attitudes, and operational practicality. Planning for management of public lands requires public participation.

Key Words: multiple use, public lands, biological feasibility, economic efficiency, economic equity, cultural acceptability, operational practicality, public participation

INTRODUCTION

The United States is the fourth largest country in the world. The six largest countries, in descending order of size, are the USSR, the People's Republic of China, Canada, the United States, Brazil, and Australia.

As a very large country, the United States includes lands of many physically different kinds: large areas of fertile cropland, extensive natural grazing lands, large areas of productive forests, magnificent national parks, seashores, swamps, deserts, bare mountain tops, and alluvial plains (Clawson, 1972). Because of this enormous diversity, generalizations about land must be made with caution. There are indeed some generalizations that can be made for land, as distinct from say, water or air; but basic facts about one kind of land may not apply to other kinds of land.

Land use necessarily involves land users. Every resident of the United States and millions of residents of other countries use U.S. land or the products of such land. This is clearly true for the food grown on our farmlands, but it is also true to a large extent for our forests and finest recreation lands. Because the users include everyone, they are people of all ages, both sexes, all racial and ethnic groups, and all income levels. All the variety and richness of the American people find expression among land users. As with land, so with users: Be cautious in making generalizations, which may not apply to everyone.

THE PUBLIC/PRIVATE DICHOTOMY

The customary distinction between public and private lands assumes or implies a simple, clear, and complete distinction between them— land is either privately owned, or it is publicly owned. But this view is not accurate because it greatly oversimplifies a complex land ownership and land use situation (Dana and Fairfax, 1980; Public Land Law Review Commission, 1970; Shands and Healy, 1977).

First of all, title to the land or title to some part of the bundle of rights which accompany land ownership may be divided for a single tract of land. For instance, the federal government owns the minerals under some 66 million acres of land, the surface of which is owned by private parties. The split ownership is currently highly important for coal in the northern Great Plains, where extensive areas of the best coal are owned by the federal government but ranchers or others own the surface. But split title exists in many other situations as well.

All "public" land (with minor exceptions) is used by private individuals. It is this private use of public land which makes extensive public land ownership acceptable or desired in a country basically dedicated to private property. But this is also the source of most of the headaches in public land management.

The terms for private use of public land vary greatly. At one extreme are the offshore oil and gas leases where the leases remain in effect as long as oil and/or gas is produced in paying quantities. This "land" is still publicly owned when the lease expires; but what is its value, when all economically recoverable petroleum has been removed? The rancher has a grazing "privilege" (as the agencies describe it) for a limited term, no more than 10 years; but, in fact, politically, the rancher cannot be displaced at the end of that term without the greatest difficulty. The family who picnics at a national forest campground has a very limited "lease" on the area, yet an exclusive one for the period it occupies the site. Wilderness designations are described as "forever," but one cannot help but wonder about the definition of this term.

In all of these relationships, one must carefully distinguish between legal and political power. A public agency or a private party may have legal power but lack political power to carry out some program or use of the land.

But the blurring of lines between public and private land arises for nominally private land as well. All "private" land in the United States is subject to some degree of public control or public influence in its private use. This is most obvious for urban and suburban land subject to zoning or other local land-use controls; but subsidies, credit incentives or limitations, and social pressures of many kinds may limit the freedom of the nominal owner to do exactly what he or she pleases with a particular tract of land.

In fact, there are many gradations of private versus public control over land use, whatever may be the legal "ownership" of the land. There is no clear and sharp line between "public" land with strongly entrenched private users and "private" land subject to rigorous and closely defined public controls.

DEFINITIONS OF SINGLE AND MULTIPLE USE

I define "use" to include any output of goods or services or any quality of the land that gives satisfaction or pleasure to the landowner or to the land user. These satisfactions and pleasures have economic value but not necessarily financial value. This definition is intentionally very broad, stated in general terms, and applicable to all kinds of land and all kinds of land-use situations.

On the basis of this definition, all land produces more than one kind of output, hence all land is multiple use. All land is watershed because rain and snow fall on all land; all land has wildlife of some form or forms; and all land has scenic or aesthetic qualities. The magnitude of these "outputs" or services may vary greatly among tracts or land, as may the quality of the outputs. The water that falls on the land may sink in, or run off, or be evaporated, with greatly varying values to prospective users; and it may be clean, pure, and cold or it may be dirty, polluted, and hot. Some uses of land do indeed preclude other uses—wilderness areas are closed to timber harvest, timber harvest destroys wilderness values, etc. The degree of compatibility of various uses varies greatly.

Whatever may be the primary use of land, some secondary outputs will be forthcoming as well. These may be desired by the landowner/ user, or he may be indifferent to them, or he may resist or oppose some secondary output. The farmer will have some (though perhaps limited) wildlife in his fields and on his farm, even if he tries to rid himself of some kinds. Or the forest may have some kinds of trees or shrubs which the owner does not want but has great difficulty getting rid of.

Many persons who speak of multiple use of land have two other considerations in mind: (1) they mean a planned combination of uses, different than would arise without some positive action; and (2) they mean more of some use in which they are particularly interested, than would have arisen as incidental to some other dominant use.

A planned multiple use, which seeks to obtain a different combination of outputs than would have arisen in its absence, necessarily involves some trade-offs—more of one kind of output and less of another. And this, in turn, necessarily involves evaluation of each kind of output, is the more of one more or less valuable than the less of another? The problems of such evaluation are difficult, and are addressed later in this chapter.

FEDERAL MULTIPLE-USE LANDS

Planned multiple-use management is far more common and far more in the public consciousness on public than on private land. At least some members of the whole public will argue that, as one of the owners of the public land, they have a right to make such uses of land as they desire. And, among the various kinds of publicly owned land, it is the lands managed by the U.S. Forest Service and the Bureau of Land Management on which planned multiple use is most important (Arizona Law Review, 1979; Brubaker, 1984; Clawson, 1983; Johnston and Emerson, 1984). Each agency operates under federal laws which dictate—even if they do not well define—multiple use as the objective. On most other federal land, such as national parks, wildlife refuges, military reservations, and others, one or a few uses are dominant; and some major uses are excluded.

The lands administered by the U.S. Forest Service and the Bureau of Land Management are used by many different groups for many purposes (see Table 3–1). The various uses are reported in terms appropriate for that use, but comparisons among uses are difficult because the units of reporting are different. Recreation clearly involves the largest number of people, but the data in Table 3–1 are for visitor days, not visitors or persons. There are no data available as to the number of different persons who made this number of visitor days. The number of visitor days somewhat exceeds the number of persons in the United States, so that, on the average, each person visited one of the areas managed by these two agencies more than once during the year. However, it is certain that many persons in the United States never visited one of these areas. Dividing the number of visitor days by four or more might yield a reasonable estimate of the number of individuals who visited one of these areas.

The number of grazing permittees on the national forests and on the grazing districts has some degree of overlap; perhaps no more than 20,000 families are involved. This seems fewer than the probable number of persons who visited these areas for outdoor recreation. However, these permittees had from 15 to 20 million animal unit months of grazing. The federal ranges are, for the most part, seasonal; private ranchers use them for a grazing season of from six weeks to five months. If the number of animal unit months is multiplied by 30, to get animal use days, then the total is about 500 million—substantially more than the number of recreation use days. Is one day of grazing for a cow as valuable or as important as one day of outdoor recreation for a human, or more so, or less so? Clearly, there is room for differences of opinion here.

As far as numbers of persons are concerned, outdoor recreation is the dominant use of the multiple-use federal lands (Clawson and Knetsch, 1966). As far as income is concerned, oil and gas production from the outer continental shelf is dominant, with well over two-thirds of all federal income from its multiple-use "lands" coming from this source.

Unfortunately, the available data do not show how much these various uses occurred on the same tracts of land and how much they were on separate but intermingled tracts of land. Informed persons know that some of the livestock grazing occurred on forested land where timber harvest might also occur; or some of the outdoor recreation—such as hunting—was on land recently harvested of timber. Not only does the available record not show the degree to which uses occurred on the same land but it also does not show the degree of conflict among uses or the degree to which one use had to be modified to accommodate another use. This kind of information is often available in local records or in the minds of persons locally operative, but national summaries of data do not exist.

The terms on which use of these multiple-use federal lands are available to the public vary greatly among the various uses, as Table 3–1 shows. At one extreme are the mining explorations; any federal land not explicitly closed to such exploration is open to anyone, without the knowledge or consent of the federal agency. At the other extreme are most timber sales and all competitive mineral leases, where the agency sets terms (but not the royalty rate for mineral leases), offers the resource for private use and development, and monitors the use and collects the funds. For all uses, the resultant use is a combination

Table 3–1
Use of Federal Lands (1980)

Activity	Agency	Approximate number of users (1,000)	Approximate area available for use (million A.)	Payment to federal government (a) (million $)	Terms for obtaining use and governing use
Grazing	FS	16	(100)	11(b)	Application by user; terms set by agency
	BLM	14	156	16(c)	Sale offering by agency; competitive bid
Timber	FS	89	92	730	
	BLM	1.8(d)	5 (e)	303(f)	
Oil and gas, onshore(g):					
Noncompetitive	BLM	105			Application and lottery; 12½% royalty
Competitive	BLM			605(h)	Advertised by agency; competitive bid; 12½% royalty
Oil and Gas, OCS	BLM	2.2	10.7 (i)	4,101	Advertised by agency; competitive bid; 16⅔% royalty

Coal	BLM	.5	1.0 (j)	32	Application; royalty fixed by agency
Other leasable minerals(g)	BLM			17	Application; royalty fixed by agency
Mining exploration	FS,BLM	unknown		0	User chooses any open areas
Recreation	FS(k)	233,549	172	18	Decision by users
	BLM(k)	64,706	447	(l)	Decision by users
Total payments			5,833		

Note: Numbers in parentheses are estimates by the author.

Source: Adapted from Table 3.3, Marion Clawson, *The Federal Lands Revisited* (Resources for the Future, Washington, D.C. 1983), p. 106. Basic data from records of agencies.

(a) Royalty terms for oil and gas specified in law; no payments for mineral exploration; all other outputs, prices and terms determined by administrative action of agency, under applicable laws.

(b) 1978;

(c) 1979;

(d) O & C only;

(e) excludes Alaska;

(f) O & C only, 1979;

(g) national forests and acquired lands have been included in BLM;

(h) public domain only, excludes acquired lands;

(i) Area under lease, total area OCS over 200 million acres;

(j) area under lease, potential area more than 11 million acres;

(k) visitor-days, not visitors, includes wilderness areas. Based on 1979 figures for BLM;

(l) not shown separately.

of private desire and public agency decision, but in different proportions for the various uses (Gates, 1968).

PLANNING MULTIPLE USE OF FEDERAL RURAL LAND

The procedures for planning the multiple use of federal rural land are necessarily complex and involve five separate kinds of professional expertise and five important kinds of factual considerations: (1) physical/biological feasibility and consequences; (2) economic efficiency; (3) economic equity, or who gains and who pays; (4) cultural acceptability, or what we choose more or less of regardless of costs; and (5) administrative practicality (Clawson, 1975). These five kinds of considerations are discussed in the sections that follow.

Physical/Biological Feasibility and Consequences

Planning the multiple use of rural federal lands—as indeed, planning the use and/or development of any natural resource for any use—should rest on the most complete, most accurate, and most relevant scientific information about the resource that can be obtained. For land, this includes information on soils, climate, present vegetation, nutrient cycles, hydrological cycles, energy balance, presence or hazard of disease, and many other factors. Each of these kinds of information may be important, even critical; and any kind of information omitted or overlooked may come to have critical importance at some later date. Since planning is concerned with the future, so must these kinds of information be concerned with the future.

Clearly, assembly and compilation of these various kinds of physical/ biological information require the professional input of many kinds of scientists: soils specialists, climatologists, ecologists, botanists, entomologists, and others, each with a special knowledge, jargon, and theoretical concepts.

It is not enough to appraise the physical/biological feasibility of various alternative lines of action; in addition, it is essential to estimate the consequences of these same alternatives. What happens next year, or next decade, or next generation if some particular action is taken? Or if it is not taken? Change is inherent in all natural situations, and it is absurd to pretend that anything will continue in the future exactly as it is today. In the modern world, humans have become major change agents, whether for "good" or for "bad," and we must consider the probable consequences of all of our actions.

This appraisal of physical/biological feasibility and consequences should be as realistic as possible. There is little gained and much may be lost by proposing some action—or in opposing some action—that simply will not yield the desired results. A dream of what could be done with oil royalties is meaningless if there is no possibility of oil development, for instance. Or it is misleading to talk about natural pine regeneration after harvest in a mixed pine-hardwood stand if, in fact, the hardwood will crowd out the pine. The list of impossible or most unlikely resource uses and developments is very long indeed.

The need will often exist to estimate the trade-offs between one output and another. If a virgin forest is harvested, this may mean the end of spotted owls in that area; but deer and other grazing animals may increase on the newly released ground vegetation. How many deer are gained at what loss of spotted owls? And so on, for many other examples of trade-offs. Trade-offs have economic dimensions, which we consider later, but they have biological dimensions also.

Physical/biological considerations may, but usually do not, involve an all-or-nothing comparison; rather, there are gradations or steps from one situation to another, as more or less of some input or some practice is introduced. The biologist should produce the equivalent of the economist's supply curve.

Last, the physical/biological analysis should include consideration of measures to mitigate effects that are considered adverse. For instance, if some disease or insect infestation threatens to injure or exterminate some plant or animal species deemed desirable, what can be done to reduce such damage or to offset it?

Economic Efficiency

Economic efficiency is an important dimension of any proposed resource use or development. What are the probable costs, and what are the probable benefits? The usual economic efficiency analysis does not consider who pays the costs and who gets the benefits; that is the concern of the next section of this chapter. The usual analysis is in terms of all costs and all benefits, on whomever the costs may fall and whomever may get the benefits.

Benefit/cost analysis is normally concerned with the future—the period typically considered in physical/biological feasibility and consequence analysis. Often the costs are incurred in the short run and the benefits hopefully flowing for some time in the future. Clearly, uncertainty is necessarily involved. Costs and benefits can be reduced to a common point in time, normally the present, by various discounting methods; but these involve a choice of interest rate, which in itself is a highly uncertain factor. The results of benefit/cost analysis may be stated in terms of a ratio between them, in terms of discounted present net values, in terms of internal rate of return, or in other ways. While these different expressions each have their particular characteristics and problems, all have basic similarities.

Many biologically and physically feasible uses of land and other natural resources are not economically efficient since the costs are greater than the values created. There is an immense volume of oil in the oil shale deposits on federal land, but thus far the cost of retrieving it has exceeded the values concerned. We could desalt sea water for irrigation to produce staple crops, but the costs are far too great, in relation to the values. For the rural federal multiple-use lands, timber can be grown commercially on many poor sites but only at costs in excess of values. In general, economic efficiency is a more restrictive criterion than is physical/biological feasibility.

Although benefit/cost analysis is widely used—and misused—in natural resource use and development, there are many fallacies or misconceptions about it, as applied to rural federal lands as well as to other natural resource situations (Howe, 1979). Some of these may be briefly considered, as follow.

First, many persons assume that the prices received for the commodities or services sold from rural federal lands are a fair measure of the full value of such goods or services. Such persons often make much of the "competitive" sale of some resource outputs, such as timber or competitive lease sales of petroleum and other minerals. But this is often a serious mistake. The competitive market of the economist does not exist; there is but one seller—the federal government—and often but one possible buyer, or at most a few. The recent commission studying leasing of federal coal-bearing lands brought this out most forcefully, that is, the conditions for a truly competitive sale are rarely present (Commission on Fair Market Value Policy for Federal Coal Leasing, 1984). A number of studies have shown that so-called competitive sales of timber from federal lands often do not produce genuine competition and presumably do not produce a full value price for the timber. Grazing fees are notoriously below a competitive market level. In any comparisons of economic efficiency of different use of rural federal lands, it is a mistake to accept uncritically the prices received from so-called competitive sales. They may simply be in error, and at the least should be studied critically.

A different and yet somewhat similar misconception or fallacy exists for those commodities or services from rural federal land which are not typically sold for a cash price: outdoor recreation, including wilderness use, visual or aesthetic values, wildlife, and even water flowing off the land. There is a real value, though not a monetary price, for such products and services. Moreover, estimates of such values can be made, which often are as accurate as the data from sales of those products sold for cash.

As long as the public in general acts in predictable ways—and not necessarily in ways the analyst thinks are rational—it is possible to make some estimate of the values people are unconsciously putting on the goods and services in question. A reliable procedure has been developed for measuring the value of outdoor recreation, based on travel and other costs recreationists are willing to incur, and upon the resulting numbers of recreation visits. As a result of such analysis, it is possible to estimate the price at which different amounts and qualities of outdoor recreation could be "sold," were an attempt made to realize significant revenue from such sales. Indeed, this is what the operator of a private campground or park does, whether he does it explicitly or more or less intuitively.

The price at which various amounts and qualities of outdoor recreation could be sold is one factor; the consumer surplus, or the amount which some persons would have paid if necessary to get the service or to retain a service long enjoyed, is another matter. For many kinds of natural resource use made possible by public (governmental) action, it is the consumer surplus that is often considered. What is the total benefit to society, regardless of who pays for it? Consumer surplus will always be larger, and often greatly larger, than possible revenues from sale or charges for resource use.

A third major misconception or fallacy about benefit/cost analysis is that decisions about natural resource use, including decisions about various uses of rural federal lands, can be made without consideration of economic values. This is a rather widespread fallacy, especially among physical and biological scientists. It is nonsense to think that economic values can be ignored; as long as anyone is forced to choose among alternatives, an economic decision has been made. Economics is concerned with decision making when wants or desires exceed means to satisfy them, which means, in practice, always. An ecologist or a silviculturist who may denounce economics as a basis for decisions will nevertheless choose one course of action in preference to another and in doing so will have made an economic choice, and implicitly an economic analysis. The real issue in natural resource management, including planned multiple use of rural federal lands, is between the best—though likely imperfect—economic analysis and something worse or less dependable.

Last, some persons have reasoned that, since a conceptually and operationally fully defensible allocation of costs among outputs from multiple-use management cannot be made, that benefit/cost analysis has no usefulness. But it is not necessary to make a cost allocation among joint outputs of a multiple-use management program. The only issue is whether the net output of the whole management program is greater or smaller with a particular output or practice included than it is with that output or practice omitted. This indeed requires estimation of many factors and likely leaves much uncertainty about the future, but a cost allocation is definitely not needed.

As one who has been involved for many years in planning and analysis of natural resource use and development, including multiple-use management of rural federal lands, my conclusion about economic analysis is to make the best economic analysis possible, looking at every item of cost and every item of benefit, but critically for each; treat the results as approximations, not as absolutes; and be guided by but not totally constrained by the answers. Economic efficiency is a goal more highly regarded by economists than it is by legislators or even by the general public. I regard economic efficiency as a highly desirable guide to decisions and actions but never sufficient alone.

Economic Equity

Because economic efficiency alone is not a sufficient guide to decisions about natural resource use and development, it must be supplemented by economic equity, or who bears the costs and who gains the benefits. In most natural resource situations, there is a substantial disassociation between time periods with major costs frequently being incurred at the beginning and benefits hopefully flowing for a considerable time in the future. Often it is the general taxpayer who bears the costs while some group, often small, gets the benefits.

A great many people, individually and in groups, will fight harder for what they regard as their fair share of benefits than they will fight for overall economic efficiency. If the general taxpayer pays most of the costs of some water development, a benefited group may gain greatly even though the overall economic efficiency is negative. "What is there in it for me?" is the common concern. It is often difficult to define what is truly fair to all parties concerned. In the case of the rural federal lands, the total costs incurred by the U.S. Forest Service and by the Bureau of Land Management in timber and grazing operations are substantially in excess of the revenues produced; and to a large extent the general taxpayer foots the bill.

For economic efficiency, there is a fairly simple test of desirability— benefits should exceed costs, and by the largest margin feasible. There is no such neat test for economic equity. One may argue that every beneficiary should pay the costs due to his or her use of federal lands; but often this is not easy to ascertain, in part because of the joint production of several outputs from the one management system. How far should management of the federal lands seek to overcome or mitigate income disparities among the user publics? There are many difficult and often highly emotional concerns here, but they must be faced in multiple-use management of the rural federal lands.

The economist is often the professional person best qualified to estimate the gains and the costs to each group, though economists are no more able to make socially desirable decisions than are others. The economist will often realize that the apparent beneficiary of some management program is not the ultimate beneficiary. Both costs and benefits may be passed onto some other person or group, and the first beneficiary may not be the ultimate one.

Cultural Acceptability

But economic efficiency and economic equity together may not serve as a basis for a final decision on natural resource use. There are many actions that people consider right and proper, almost irrespective of costs. For instance, there are some people strongly opposed to clear-cutting of timber and no amount of biological analysis, consideration of economic efficiency, or economic equity will overcome their opposition. Others feel strongly about the "preservation" of wild and free-roaming horses and burros, and no biological analysis of the inevitable consequences, or of the economic costs and benefits, or of the gainers and losers, will deter them from their advocacy. There is a large opposition to nuclear power in the United States, much of it impervious to the kinds of analysis discussed thus far.

People have philosophical or ideological attitudes and positions, formed out of the general culture in which they were born and raised. Most people are unaware of their own cultural biases and positions, as noted they hold these views because they seem "natural." Someone from a different culture is often better able to describe and appraise such ideological or philosophical positions than is a person who is a member of the group that holds them. Those who do not hold a particular set of attitudes often regard such attitudes as irrational, whereas the holder considers them natural.

Cultural attitudes are often hard to identify, describe meaningfully, and take account of in natural resource planning, yet they must be considered for planning and management of the rural federal lands, no less than for other natural resource situations.

Some conservationists seem to feel that their motives in seeking use of federal lands are purer or higher or more noble than are the motives of those groups that seek financial gain from federal land use. It is a serious mistake to assume that one's rivals or competitors are somehow less highly motivated than one's self. The rancher grazing livestock on federal land may value his role in supplying the nation's meat as highly as does the wildlife specialist value his role in protecting wildlife on the same area. No group has a monopoly on virtue or high motivation.

Administrative Practicality

Last, the administrative practicality of any plan or proposed program must be considered. Can we (collectively) actually do what we have decided we wish to do? Many planners and analysts are poor administrators or managers, and many of the latter have little regard for formal plans developed by others. Often there is a serious hiatus between plans and actual operations on the ground.

Does some proposed plan of action call for better trained and more able personnel than can be found, especially at the salaries that can be paid? Or is the planned procedure so complicated that, in practice, it will break down or not even be tried by persons on the ground? Does the planned line of action assume a freedom from "politics" or from intervention by some members of the public, which is most unlikely to exist? One could go on, listing or describing other questionable or unrealistic aspects of plans.

I believe there is nothing gained, and much may be lost, by proposing some line of action which simply is impractical of realization. Such an unrealizable line, though perhaps perfect by some standards, is likely to make impossible more modest but clearly positive accomplishments. Failure not only discredits those most directly involved but also alienates those who had hoped for more.

This general matter of administrative practicality arises in specific form with the U.S. Forest Service and Bureau of Land Management planning for multiple use of rural federal lands. Both agencies are directed by recent legislation to undertake such multiple-use planning, but the results to date have hardly been wholly satisfactory (Dana and Fairfax, 1980). Plans are so slow to be formulated, are so expensive, and are so complex that personnel on the ground have difficulty in understanding them. Some have argued that this planning to date has been worthless or worse. At the least, it is a matter of concern to all planners and analysts.

Synthesis of Five Approaches

The synthesis of these five approaches of physical/biological feasibility and consequences, economic efficiency, economic equity, cultural acceptability, and administrative practicality is very difficult but necessary. These considerations involve different mind-sets of their practitioners, different philosophies, different theories, and different kinds of data or information. It would be extremely difficult, if not impossible, to devise a formula which combined all five into a single mathematical result; even if such a formula could be devised, it would be impossible to simultaneously maximize the effect of each of the five variables. A different approach is necessary.

The problem is further complicated because of the interactions among these five variables. I have described them as if each were separate, yet in fact each affects to some degree each of the others. If some new line of action is highly profitable—the economic efficiency is high—then cultural reluctance toward it may well give way. For instance, new foods or new varieties of familiar foods often meet cultural opposition in some area, yet if food production is doubled or more by the introduction of the new food or new variety, people shortly will come to accept the new food. If some new biological process promises much better results than any former process, some means will be found to make the new process administratively practical. And so on, for other pairings of considerations. But all this complicates further an already complicated process.

The practical course, it seems to me, is negotiation and trade-offs with each party seeking as much of what it wants as possible, yet conceding something to other parties. The analogy is closer to labor-management bargaining than it is to computer-dominated maximizing or optimizing. Each of the specialist groups may have to accept some result as tolerable but not ideal or, as the economists say it, to satisfy rather than to maximize. This, in essence, is the political process at its best—to achieve the most possible for each party at the least cost to each.

Public Participation

Nowadays there is general agreement that the public should be consulted—indeed, involved—with natural resource and environmental planning (Culhane, 1981). The U.S. Forest Service and the Bureau of Land Management are under strict instructions, in their enabling legislation, to involve the public in their planning. Like so many ideas that sound fine in general terms, implementation raises its own special set of problems.

In the first place, if the public is to be involved, it should be, as far as possible, the whole public and not merely those parts of the public that are most aggressive about being involved, nor just that part of the public with which the government official is on the friendliest terms, nor just that part of the whole public that lives near the lands in question. The Forest Service and the Bureau of Land Management together incur an annual cash deficit of over $1 billion, which must be made up by the taxpayers of the country—about four dollars each. What do the taxpayers who never do, or perhaps cannot, use these rural multiple-use federal lands get for their four dollars, and who speaks for them? The public agency personnel have a clear responsibility to involve as much of the whole public as can be reached or is interested, but the various interest groups have a responsibility to get involved too (Sedjo, 1983; Shands, 1979).

The public should be given an opportunity to be involved in the planning of rural multiple-use federal lands right from the beginning of the planning process, not merely midway of the planning or at the end. The participation may sometimes best be informal, when there can be a give-and-take of ideas, rather than in a formal way when various groups may be posturing and speaking for the record as much as genuinely seeking solutions. But a formal hearing at some stage may be necessary, not only to comply with the law but to give a chance for any interested person or group to make a formal statement for the record.

If the public is to participate in planning for rural multiple-use federal lands, then it must be given a fair opportunity to do so effectively. This means that relevant information should be easily available in understandable form, that meetings should be held at readily accessible places and times, and that the public should not be asked to react on matters where they cannot possibly be adequately informed. Moreover, this should be done with enough time for consideration and preparation of adequate responses.

However desirable it is that the public participate in planning, and however well the planning process has been carried out, in the end it is the public official who must decide. The public can help, but it is the official who must take the responsibility for the decision and for the subsequent action. It is only he or she whom the executive branch, the Congress, and the courts can and will hold responsible. No advisory group can be sued for bad advice if things go awry. However influential any interest group or combination of interest groups may be, it or they are advisors, not deciders. There are, of course, plenty of examples, not only in resource management but elsewhere, when these roles have not been respected, but in the end any attempt by advisory groups to get into the direct line of decision making nearly always makes for trouble.

Some persons have been concerned that the public land and resource manager who is forced to consult the public has thereby lost professional stature. This need not be so. The astute federal resource manager consults all the public interest groups, serves as a mediator or synthesizer of conflicting views rather than as a protagonist of any one view, and in the end can achieve a major professional output and be recognized for it by all parties. But he or she cannot escape responsibility for decision (LeMaster, 1984).

One of the most troublesome questions is whether or not the interest groups that have offered their advice—and that seem to have accepted compromises with other interest groups—will really honor their commitments when the going gets rough. Will they instead seek to make an end run to the courts or to the legislatures? Every interest group can recount some instances in which it believes bargains it struck with other interest groups were repudiated. Trust and distrust are as important in natural resource management as they are in international relations. In planning of rural multiple-purpose federal lands, it is probably hopeless to seek an enforceable agreement among various interest groups, but the public participation process may produce a compromise that all can and will live with. At least, we can hope so.

BIBLIOGRAPHY

Arizona Law Review. 1979. Vol. 21, no. 2 is devoted to a consideration of management of federal lands.

Brubaker, Sterling, ed. 1984. *Rethinking the Federal Lands.* Washington, D.C.: Resources for the Future.

Clawson, Marion. 1983. *The Federal Lands Revisited.* Washington: Resources for the Future.

———. 1975. *Forests for Whom and for What?* Baltimore: Johns Hopkins University Press.

———. 1972. *America's Land and Its Uses.* Baltimore: Johns Hopkins Press.

Clawson, Marion, and Jack L. Knetsch. 1966. *Economics of Outdoor Recreation.* Baltimore: Johns Hopkins University Press.

Commission of Fair Market Value Policy for Federal Coal Leasing. 1984. *Report.* Washington, D.C.: Commission on Fair Market Value Policy for Federal Coal Leasing.

Culhane, Paul J. 1981. *Public Lands Politics—Interest Group Influence on the Forest Service and the Bureau of Land Management.* Washington, D.C.: Resources for the Future.

Dana, Samuel T., and Sally K. Fairfax. 1980. *Forest and Range Policy,* 2d ed. New York: McGraw-Hill.

Gates, Paul W. 1968. *History of Public Land Law Development.* Washington, D.C.: U.S. Government Printing Office.

Howe, Charles W. 1979. *Natural Resource Economics—Issues, Analysis, and Policy.* New York: John Wiley and Sons.

Johnston, George M., and Peter M. Emerson, eds. 1984. *Public Lands and the U.S. Economy—Balancing Conservation and Development.* Boulder, CO: Westview Press.

LeMaster, Dennis C. 1984. *Decade of Change: The Remaking of Forest Service Statutory Authority During the 1970s.* Westport, CT: Greenwood Press.

Public Land Law Review Commission. 1970. *One Third of the Nation's Land.* Washington, D.C.: U.S. Government Printing Office.

Sedjo, Roger A., ed. 1983. *Governmental Interventions, Social Needs, and the Management of U.S. Forests.* Washington, D.C.: Resources for the Future.

Shands, William E. 1979. *Federal Resource Lands and Their Neighbors.* Washington, D.C.: The Conservation Foundation.
Shands, William E., and Robert G. Healy. 1977. *The Lands Nobody Wanted.* Washington, D.C.: The Conservation Foundation.

4

NATURE PROTECTION AND APPRECIATION: A NEW OR OLD CONCEPT?

M. Brock Evans

ABSTRACT

Contrary to some assumptions there is a long history of appreciation of wild nature in American culture. There is an equal willingness to work to protect it. Any discussion or allocation of public lands must take these cultural factors into account.

Key Words: conservation, wilderness, spiritual, history, parks, multiple-use, public land

INTRODUCTION

The contributors to this book are frequently noted for the considerable thought they have given over the course of their careers to the pressing problems of our environment in general and, hopefully, the subject of this book—multiple use of public lands—in particular.

As the vice president of a large grassroots environmental organization in Washington, D.C. (in other words, a lobbyist) I wrestle with questions of public lands administration and legislation every day. It is in a world of bustling corridors and hurried whispered conversations, jangling telephones, and constant interruptions, and in a world of surges of people, each pressing their own case where the weightiest of decisions affecting many lives and the well being of millions are made in minutes, and sometimes without much thought.

For better or for worse—most of the time I think for better—this has been the world I have lived and moved in for the past 20 years. And, in our political system, this is the way most decisions about public lands are made, and most policies are finally set by the U.S. Congress, which is the final arbiter of such things.

My world is quite different from the world of the think tanks, academia, and the like, where all the pieces seem to fit together. In this latter world time constraints seem not as great and learned people deal rationally in nice settings. That is quite different from my work, and the world where I normally work. Both worlds are important; both are real.

POLITICS AS THE ULTIMATE LAND-USE REALITY

I know it is fashionable to say that the world of Washington is unreal, that it doesn't reflect what America is all about, and it certainly doesn't reflect the realities out there on the ground when we talk about public lands. But I submit just the opposite: This is the ultimate reality. I submit, further, that, while "what is out there on the ground" is obviously extremely important, public land managers or policy makers who ignore the political part of the equation—with all its attendant weighting of value systems, emotions, and other intangible factors—ignore the most fundamental part of any effort necessary to achieve satisfactory management of these lands.

In spite of the demands and pressures of this world in which I have moved and lived for two decades—or perhaps indeed because of them—I have over this time given considerable thought to the questions being raised in this book, as well as the factors so expertly and clearly laid out in Chapter 3 by Marion Clawson.

Finally, after sitting through so many hearings, covering every aspect of public lands allocation and management, not only in Washington, D.C., but everywhere across the nation, I have been struck again and again by the intensity, the passion behind the subject matter, a passion often, in my view, far out of proportion to any specific resource at stake at any given point and time. "What is the source of this passion?," I have asked myself. "And does it tell us something about what the public lands really are to us as an American people, and how, therefore, we must approach them if we are to manage them successfully?"

PUBLIC LANDS ARE MUCH MORE THAN COMMODITIES

This factor of passion has been too often missing in any discussion of this type at gatherings of experts, in Washington or anywhere else. I believe that we must devise a better way to take this factor of passion into account if we are to have a successful approach to our public lands for the next century. This is what I want to address in this chapter.

The subject matter of almost any meeting I have attended on the subject of public lands seems to approach our lands in terms of their value or usefulness as producers of certain tangible and specific commodities, such as forest products, minerals, acre-feet of water, quantities of huntable game, and even recreation visitor days. I believe that even Marion Clawson's chapter, as fine as it is, tends to approach public lands management questions in similar abstract terminology.

Let me say at the outset that neither I personally, nor we in the Audubon Society—or probably any other environmental organization— have any argument with the notion that our public lands can, and indeed do, produce large quantities of timber, minerals, oil and gas, game, and recreation. That is the law, and we have supported the law. We have supported the Multiple-Use Act, and have consistently pressed federal agencies to manage the land according to multiple-use principles.

We have certainly differed with them and with industry on definitions of multiple use, and it is no secret that we have believed that, for the entire time of existence of our public lands system, the emphasis, in practice if not in statute, has been overwhelmingly in favor of commodity production. It has been so at the expense of the more intangible, but nevertheless real values such as nature appreciation, the wilderness and its sense of space and vastness, the opportunity to be in contact with that type of landscape, and, therefore, the feelings and emotions of our ancestors who first came here. The law states that the public lands ought to produce certain commodities, and we support that law.

Nevertheless, I believe there can be too much attention to the commodity aspect of the public lands in discussions such as these, and that such discussions can take us too far away from what is indeed the "reality out there on the ground." The public lands are something far more than just producers of certain outputs to be factored into the computers and equations, then to be considered by decision makers.

THE SPIRITUAL SIGNIFICANCE OF PUBLIC LANDS

After nearly a quarter of a century of being out there on the ground and walking through the lands, and after over two decades of listening to the people at public hearings, in their towns and cities, and on the trail, I believe that the public lands have a deep and profound, even spiritual, meaning to us as a whole people. They have everything to do with our psyche as Americans. Some of these "intangible" concepts already are so deeply ingrained in us that they have become forever a part of who we are, and are not to be tampered with in our national life. Let me cite some examples.

First, it is unthinkable to consider selling off these lands in the interest of "economic efficiency," or "privatization." The Reagan administration tried this just a few years ago, and suffered one of the most humiliating defeats of its regime.

Second, it is unthinkable not to have public use of an access to the public lands. This concept, which began in the earliest days of the frontier, is strikingly different from other free-world countries with similar traditions and large public land holdings. For example, in Canada the provincial governments, which have the largest land holdings, traditionally lease out large tracts to private companies for exploitation, mostly timber purposes, and the public has only a limited right to use the lands. This concept would be politically unacceptable here.

Third, it is unthinkable for any public land manager in the United States to approach the question of planning for his or her lands without assuming that the public would have an enormous input, opportunity to speak and be heard, access to all relevant documents, and to have its views actually incorporated into the final document. This again distinguishes us greatly from countries even with similar political traditions.

Finally, with all the "unthinkables" noted above, something else has happened: It has become more thinkable to move farther away from the notion that the public lands are primarily there to produce exploitable commodities for the personal profit of private corporations. While this concept will always be with us, and it should be, the idea that the public lands hold values of the deepest spiritual and symbolic significance to Americans as a part of themselves is truly taking hold. For example, a poll conducted in 1977 by the American Forest Institute, the educational arm of the forest products industry, found that almost two-thirds of the American people felt there should be no logging whatsoever in any of the national forests, not just the wilderness areas and parks.

I submit that if any of our discussions are to have truly productive significance and results, they must take these fundamental facts, these fundamental "thinkables" and "unthinkables," into account. I submit further that no planning exercise by any public lands manager will succeed in having lasting impact—indeed, no planning exercise will stick—unless it takes them into account.

WHERE DID THIS LOVE FOR OUR LANDS COME FROM?

Let us discuss this just a little further. Contrary to the thinking of many, a love for the lands—and appreciation for their attractions and power over our spirits—did not begin with the great Earth Day upheavals of the late 1960s and early 1970s. In its articulate form, this feeling has been around since the beginning of the republic itself; in a deeper sense, probably from the time the first European settlers arrived to carve homes out of the wilderness.

Early settlers' writings, of course, are full of the notion that the wilderness—and all it represented—was a savage, hostile thing to be conquered and civilized; but the constant contact with the frontier over the next 300 years seemed somehow to arouse feelings of love as well as hate, awe and wonder as well as disgust, reverence as well as fear. Thus, it was a century and a half later that a botanist named William Bartram traveled through the then-virgin country of the southern Appalachians, marveling at its beauty and fertility, lamenting its passage, pleading for its protection.

As the new country was born and began to feel its own sense of national pride, other American writers came quickly to realize that in our wilderness we had something special and unique, something that the other "effete" cultures across the ocean could never hope to duplicate. As early as 1786, Abigail Adams, in one of her famous letters wrote, "Do you know that European birds have not half the melody of ours, nor is their fruit half so sweet, nor their flowers half so fragrant, nor their manners half so pure, nor their people half so virtuous?" (Nash, 1982).

Other writers such as William Cullen Bryant and James Fenimore Cooper picked up the theme, which the romantic movement of the 1820s and 1830s expounded more fully: The American Wilderness, being more "natural" than just "nature," therefore was closer to God than anything in Europe, and therefore provided greater inspiration for the arts and literature (Nash, 1982). "I know of nothing more splendid than a forest of the west, standing in its original integrity, adorned with the exuberant beauties of a powerful vegetation and crowned with the honors of a venerable age ... " said the romanticist James Hall (Nash, 1982).

These early writings were given another kind of expression in art, through the evocative landscapes of the Hudson River school of painting; and they in turn opened the way for philosophers such as Thoreau and Emerson to rationalize these emerging feelings into the philosophical language of the day. "In wildness is the preservation of the world," said Thoreau in 1849 (Nash, 1982); and this articulated cry was taken up by a host of journalists and writers at mid-century who, viewing the rapid conquest of the West by pioneering settlements, did a series of articles in national magazines pleading that some large reserve be set aside, so that future generations could always know the power and the majesty of the landscapes that then existed in the wilderness of the West.

Clearly, the constant contact with the wild frontier of the public domain had by then transformed us as a people, made us no longer

Europeans or Asians or Africans but something wholly different and unique: Americans. All sensed it, all knew it, all were proud of the new race we were forming; and all knew instinctively that it had something to do with the character of the American land itself.

Thus, the next step, which has seemed so large, was really but a natural progression. In 1872, the conservative Republican President U. S. Grant signed into law a bill creating a 2-million-acre national park in the mysterious region of the Yellowstone of the central Rocky Mountains. This was a unique concept in the history of the world; and the language of the statute itself, " . . . there is hereby created, as a permanent pleasuring ground for the enjoyment of the American people . . . " tells us something about not only our character, but also our reverence for what the public lands have come to mean to us and to our willingness to do something about it. The idea that something so remote—far more remote to them than anything in Alaska is to us today—should be set aside just as it is, with the idea that it could be enjoyed as it is, was truly a uniquely American notion.

We all know what has come after that: An expansion and enlargement of the park system into the greatest, most expansive, and most truly protected of any in the world; a wildlife refuge system just as large; a national wilderness preservation system, even more protected in some ways, just as large; a wild and scenic river system; and a host of state and local preserves.

Nearly all of these vast acreages of protected landscapes were created out of the public lands; and nearly always there was a bitter struggle between park-wilderness proponents and those who saw the public lands in the more traditional commercial exploitation sense. Indeed, the very first assault was mounted in the Yellowstone itself, against the new park, exactly one century ago.

An attempt was made to place a railroad across the park to foster a mineral development, and the issue was fiercely debated in Congress. Representative Payson of Illinois outlined the traditional feeling that had governed our land policies until then: "I cannot understand the sentiment which favors the retention of a few buffalos to the development of mining interests amounting to millions of dollars." But Representative Cox of New York rejoined that the park had to be protected to preserve " . . . all that gives elevation and grace to human nature, by the observation of the works of physical nature." He was followed by Representative McAdoo of New Jersey, who disputed the popular notion that the park existed just to preserve a few specific curiosities, with an attack on the proposed railroad's impact on wilderness. He asked Congress to " . . . prefer the beautiful and sublime to heartless mammon and the greed of capital."

Thus, the lines were drawn a century ago between those who valued the public lands for their commercial potential and those who saw a different—deeper perhaps, and certainly more spiritual—significance. Battles between these two forces, and the institutions that represent them, have been almost beyond count in the intervening century: Hetchy Dam in Yosemite, creation of the National Forest Reserves, dams in Dinosaur and Grand Canyon, logging in the last wild places of the Cascades as well as the Olympics and the southern swamps, the boundary waters of Minnesota, the northern Rockies, mines in the Great Basin, grazing in the high desert wilderness, and prospecting and subsidized logging roads in Alaska.

And I would say further that, being Americans all, each of us has within ourselves a larger or smaller portion of each of these twin strains of our culture: The urge to exploit potential commercial riches and enrich ourselves from the alleged "treasure house" of our public lands and also a deep love, affection, even reverence for these our lands, their sublime landscapes, the vast sweep of the mountains across the horizon, the sound of the wind sighing high up in the trees, the murmur of a stream deep in the forest, the sunlight dancing on the shining waters of our great rivers.

CONCLUSION

And that perhaps explains why, after a century of clashes between the contending interests, more and more land continues to be set aside for essentially noncommercial purposes in the deepest sense. That also explains, I believe, why institutions such as the one I speak for and represent continue to grow in numbers and in political power. That also explains why we have yet ever more planning and "planning processes" imposed by the federal agencies as they attempt to balance the interests as best they can. Formerly, we had little or no planning, and mostly a carryover of the old assumptions that the public lands were to be used for private profit. The planning processes were imposed by pressure from without, and not from the commercial industries who had so long benefited from the old ways.

I can understand how it might be frustrating to those who had once enjoyed relatively free license to extract their products from public lands, relatively unhindered. But that will no more be the case, and we will do well to never forget this essential spiritual component of the American public lands, and the reverence for them that each of us feels deep in our own hearts, whether we are environmentalists, representatives of industry, or in the academic world. We are all Americans.

BIBLIOGRAPHY

"An Act to Set Apart a Certain Tract of Land Lying Near the Headwaters of the Yellowstone River as a Public Park." 17 Stat. 32. 1872.
84 *Congressional Record* 150, 152–54. 1886.
Nash, Roderick. 1982. *Wilderness and the American Mind*, 3d ed. New Haven: Yale University Press, pp. 59, 68–69, 75–78, 84, 97, 302.

5

NATIONAL FOREST PLANNING: LOOKING FOR HARMONY

Mary Lou Franzese

ABSTRACT

National forest planning is an example of multiple use as the concept is being interpreted and applied to a major component of the nation's rural public lands. The history of the U.S. Forest Service planning is briefly reviewed, and a systems approach is used to describe the current process. Observed planning problems are discussed and suggestions made for changing planning emphasis from resource conflicts to resource compatibility.

Key Words: national forest planning, multiple use, U.S. Forest Service, harmonious, coordinated management, Systems Age Thinking

PREFACE

This chapter is purposefully modest in scope. It looks at only one (albeit significant) portion of the multiple-use puzzle—land-use planning on the national forests—from a fairly narrow point of view, that of a local resource planning practitioner, Forest Service observer, and public involvement participant from the timber industry in northern Idaho. It focuses less on the long-term need for or desirability of sweeping policy changes in favor of the immediate question, "What do we do with what we've got?"

The discussion is informal, and given that the current round of forest planning is incomplete, it is speculative. Examples are drawn from local and personal experience, with implications proffered for larger application. Hopefully, it is thought-provoking, generating some measure of heat if not light.

INTRODUCTION

The National Forest Management Act (NFMA) and the planning process it directs have been called "the most adventurous incursion into the on-the-ground activities of the United States Forest Service" (Wilkinson and Anderson, 1985) and "the most extensive, comprehensive and detailed effort of land use planning ... ever ... attempted in the Free World" (Zivnuska, 1980). The 1976 law and process have also been likened to "riding a bicycle while you're trying to build it," a congressionally spawned "monster," and "the WPPSS of the Forest Service." It is instructive, and probably not surprising, that the more disparaging characterizations come not from the legal or academic communities but from the people intimate with its inherent frustrations, those people trying to make the process work at the local forest level.

At the very least, NFMA is a huge experiment in multiple-use planning and fertile ground for examining the concept and practice of multiple use on a major component of this nation's rural public lands.

The national forests are no small potatoes. The NFMA plans, the legal and technical blueprints for managing the national forests, will be of widespread importance to the nation's public (and private) land base, resources, economy, and society. The national forests cover some 191 million acres in 45 states, support half the standing softwood timber inventory in the nation, boast outstanding wilderness, scenic, and wildlife values, and are a major source of recreation, energy reserves, and mineral deposits (U.S. Forest Service, 1984). The national forests provide economic sustenance to hundreds of communities and are part of our nation's social fabric, whether one works and lives in the woods or has never crossed a forest boundary.

The U.S. Forest Service is charged with the task of producing 155 forest plans. What at first blush may seem a straightforward and logical process is anything but that. It is more like a complex living organism and a moving target. Multiple use is an integral part of the process; the plans must interpret and, ostensibly, implement multiple use in land-use decisions. Examples of the problems and opportunities of wrestling with multiple-use planning considerations and translating them to on-the-ground action are taken from personal experience in northern Idaho.

AN OLD GAME WITH CHANGING RULES

Planning on the national forests is nothing new. Administratively directed planning has been part of what became the Forest Service since

1898,[1] seven years before the agency had jurisdiction over the nation's "forest reserves." Early "working plans" for owners of private timber-lands, and later the forest reserves, established utilitarian and protective planning traditions for the agency (Wilkinson and Anderson, 1985).

The Forest Service continued to emphasize planning as a regular agency activity carried out by local Forest Service personnel over the next four decades. Plans were developed not only for timber and range but for daily activities, appropriations requests, and beginning in the 1920s and 1930s, for recreation and wilderness. There were even early, sporadic efforts at more comprehensive, national level planning and, following World War II, local composite plans (addressing various re-sources and management areas). These plans and management deci-sions were for the most part based on intuitive judgments by local line officers as to the best management for each part of the forest (Wilkinson and Anderson, 1985).

With passage of the Multiple Use Sustained Yield Act (MUSY Act) in 1960, Congress affirmed the Forest Service theretofore administrative policy of managing the national forests for various compatible (and sometimes competing) uses in perpetuity. The act directs the agency to manage for five multiple uses—range, wildlife, recreation, timber, and watershed—and to manage them for sustained yield. The MUSY Act defines "multiple use" to mean:

...the management of all the various renewable surface resources of the na-tional forests so that they are *utilized in the combination that will best meet the needs of the American people; that some land will be used for less than all of the resources; and harmonious and coordinated management of the various resources, each with the other,* without impairment of the productivity of the land, with consideration being given to the relative values of the various resources, *and not necessarily the combination that will give the greatest dollar for the greatest unit output* (emphasis added).

Forest Service planning took several different forms following pas-sage of the MUSY Act. In the early 1960s, the agency began writing functional plans for separate resources and also experimented with zoning of land uses.

Subsequent legislation passed in fairly rapid succession in the 1960s, and the 1970s further changed the scope and dramatically increased the complexity of planning on federal lands.[2]

The Wilderness Act and the National Environmental Policy Act of 1969 (NEPA) in particular profoundly affected Forest Service planning. In addition to mandatory wilderness protection of areas specified by Congress, the Wilderness Act set into motion a series of studies to inventory roadless lands and recommend potential areas for wilderness designation. Five years later, Congress passed NEPA, a law that has provided a tool box full of legal monkey wrenches for those with antimanagement agendas for the national forests.

NEPA is a "procedural law" that lays out a set of hoops federal agencies must jump through to arrive at a decision affecting the "human environment." In the 19 years since its passage, new "hoops" have been repeatedly advanced in the courts, particularly in sympathetic jurisdictions. Once these hoops have been recognized, the strategy has been to raise the "hoops" higher, making jumping through them increasingly difficult and complex.

NEPA has had at least three other important effects. First, it has changed the complexion of the Forest Service by introducing the interdisciplinary approach to planning and opening the doors to a flood of experts representing a wide variety of disciplines from archaeology to hydrology. Second, NEPA has dramatically increased the costs, in dollars and time, of agency planning and decision making. NEPA "hoops" such as environmental assessments (EA) and environmental impact statements (EIS) can take years to complete and, if successfully challenged through administrative appeals or the courts, years to redo. Third, NEPA also increased the role of other agencies and the public in the planning process. Public involvement in the business of the Forest Service has mushroomed under NEPA regulations.

The Forest Service sought to comply with NEPA through unit plans which generally classified forestlands into land-use zones and were developed under a predecessor of the NFMA hierarchy of planning, including regional planning area guides for subdivisions of each region. For administrative purposes, national forests lands are subdivided into nine regions, each of which is made up of national forests.

Up to 1974, Congress had seldom directly intruded into Forest Service planning and management activities. The Resources Planning Act of 1974 (RPA) and NFMA changed that historical relationship. Though RPA discusses "land management plans for use on units of the National Forest System" using a systematic interdisciplinary approach, it is really most concerned with national-level planning. RPA set into motion a national planning cycle in which the Forest Service first assesses the national picture of renewable resource supply and demand, and then uses this assessment to develop a program for renewable resource management on the national forests to meet the nation's needs.

NFMA, passed two years after RPA, amends the earlier statute. NFMA grew out of a legal challenge to clearcutting and out of a larger challenge to the agency's professional judgment in managing the forests and, specifically, timber harvesting practices. It reflects its controversial origins.

Passage of NFMA, rather than reducing controversy, has enlarged the social, economic, political, and legal battlefield, creating new procedural and substantive issues as well as potential legal vulnerabilities for the agency. Because the ultimate product is a legal document developed under a complex system of laws, regulations, agency policy, and case law—as well as a plan—the role of the judiciary was potentially elevated by its passage.

Multiple-use planning and management under NFMA might better be called "multiple-systems" planning in which the resource base itself is only one subsystem in the process, interacting with other dynamic and interdependent social, political, judicial, and technical systems of influence and change. In the time since the first NFMA regulations were adopted in 1979, once optimistic participants have come to seriously doubt that the system can work at all, and fear it will fall back into the lap of Congress.

LIFE INSIDE THE "MONSTER"

If you visited with a member of a local Forest Service interdisciplinary planning team (ID team) on Monday, there is no guarantee that same person will be there to answer questions on Friday. ID team members and others who upon going into NFMA planning thought that it would be a logical, straightforward process were, it turns out, living in a dream world.

The timber industry, for example, approached the new planning process with cautious optimism. Industry reports on the planning process express hopes that, for the first time, planning on the forest level would be designed to implement RPA program goals, tighten local forest accountability, fully display resource management opportunities existing before application of discretionary restrictions, and evaluate innovative management options. There were certainly apprehensions expressed too, but the overall tone tended to be positive.

Several years later, it is a different story. In a speech to the Forest Service, John Hall of National Forest Products Association stated:

As we approach the final phases of forest planning, it is becoming increasingly apparent that the effort is simply not leading to the consensus about resolutions to forest management controversies that Congress hoped it would.

From our perspective, the planning process threatens significant reductions in the supply of raw material....

At the risk of sounding bellicose, let me assure you of two things. First, we are watching the development of final plans in all regions. Second, we do know how to defend our interests. If necessary, we will stand squarely in front of what you perceive to be the path of least resistance (Hall, 1986).

Attitudes shifted from optimism to frustration and sharp words. Forest Service employees, just shy of 20 years service, were "jumping ship." What has been happening since 1979? Are the multiple-use questions insolvable through NFMA? Is it possible for the system to work at all?

THE PLANNING PROCESS IN BRIEF

The forest planning process is complex at best. In its most simplistic form under NFMA and NEPA, it requires the forest to complete ten major steps [35 CFR 219.12 (b)-(k)]:

1. Identification of purpose and need
2. Planning criteria development
3. Inventory of data and information collection
4. Analysis of the management situation
5. Formulation of alternatives
6. Estimate effects of alternatives
7. Evaluation of alternatives
8. Preferred alternative recommendation
9. Plan approval
10. Monitoring and evaluation

Following the planning steps and NEPA requirements results first in a Proposed Plan and Draft Environmental Impact Statement (DEIS) which are subject to public review. After evaluating public comments on the draft documents, the Plan and Final EIS are written, approved, and released with a "record of decision" stating the rationale for selection of the final management direction. After 30 days before the public, the plan is implemented. Administrative appeals may be filed and other action (for example, petition for stay of implementation) taken. Once the administrative appeals process is exhausted, the plan may be litigated.

"MULTIPLE SYSTEMS" VERSUS "MULTIPLE USE"

Key phrases in RPA/NFMA describing the character of the planning process include: "the management of the nation's renewable resources is highly complex and the uses, demand for, and supply of the various resources are subject to change over time" [Section 2(1)]; and later in the statute, "In the development and maintenance of land management plans for use on units of the National Forest System, the Secretary shall use a *systematic, interdisciplinary* approach to achieve *integrated* consideration of physical, biological, economic and other sciences" [Section 6(b)] (emphasis added).

The Forest Service must not just "consider" multiple uses, they must recognize, manage, and adapt to changes in the resource itself, changes in the level and complexity of demands our society makes, and integrate the social, economic, biological, and other factors affecting the forest, all at one time. NFMA represents a distinct shift from seeing the national forests as divisible into "uses" or independent functions, as reflected by the MUSY Act, to seeing them as integrated systems. The agency is being forced to begin to think, model, and act in terms of systems, all of which are interdependent, interactive, and dynamic.

This change is analogous to a transition underway in the industrial world. Ackoff (1972) and Trist (1981) describe this transition as a shift from the Machine Age or paradigm to that of the Systems Age. There are distinct intellectual and technological differences between the two.

Machine Age thinking rests on the mechanistic notion that everything humans perceive, experience, touch, or feel is made up of parts, and that everything is ultimately made up of indivisible parts or ultimate elements. The world is conceived of as a "machine operating in accordance with *unchanging* laws which were dictated by the structure of the world ... the world is like a hermetically sealed clock—it keeps ticking away without change over time in accordance with the laws that are derived from the structure of the clock" (Ackoff, 1972) (emphasis added).

The most powerful mode of thinking is assumed to be analysis, defined as explaining things by the behavior of their parts. A problem can be broken down into a set of solvable problems, the component problems solved and then assembled into a solution as a whole. Optimizing the solution for the parts optimizes the solution for the whole. There is also assumed to be a strict separation of the objective and subjective aspects of knowledge and reality (Garcia, 1985), and all phenomena can be explained by simple linear chains of cause and effect.

Systems Age thinking is radically different. First, it represents a shift from a preoccupation with the parts of which things are made to a preoccupation with the "whole" and the larger "whole" of which it is a part. Systems Age thinking also assumes that the performance of the whole is not the summation of the performance of the parts, but is a function of the relationships between the performance of parts. Problems are seen as interacting and interdependent sets (or subsystems) within a world that is uncertain and ever changing.

Because there is constant change, systems themselves must learn and adapt. Planning is used to solve sets of problems—what Ackoff calls "messes"—as interdependent and interactive in a context of uncertainty, and depends on the ability to develop technology capable of serving that purpose. Garcia (1985) defines systems planning as "designing a desirable future," where planning becomes "predominantly synthesizing, not analyzing."

One consequence of uncertainty and rapid change in the system is that experience may no longer be the best teacher. Experimentation that recognizes uncertainty may be a better fit.

FOREST SERVICE PLANNING: ONE FOOT IN EACH AGE

Looking at the Forest Service in terms of these two models helps characterize problems and identify opportunities for improving the NFMA process and plans. The Forest Service is attempting to perform a complex systems task with one foot planted squarely in each way of thinking.

The agency is but one subsystem interacting (within the "whole" of the larger NFMA planning system) with other subsystems—legal, sociopolitical, technological, and physical-biological—all of which are interdependent, interactive, and changing over time. Each of these subsystems affects the performance of the whole; each is reflected in the character and quality of what is being produced in the planning process.

Legal Subsystem

The legal subsystem is defined by and changed through legislative action, judicial review, Forest Service interpretation, and interactions with the sociopolitical subsystem.

For example, lobbying for new laws and use of judicial review are primary strategies of environmental groups seeking to stop, regulate, or otherwise influence Forest Service actions. Arnold (1985) describes this strategy as follows:

Environmentalist attorneys are furiously ambitious, not to follow the law, but to create it, to carve out new fields of theory, to innovate using the tools of lobbying and litigation, to create a whole new corpus of statutory and case law reflecting environmental ideologies.

As Wilkinson and Anderson (1985) point out, NFMA is fertile territory for just this kind of strategy.

Courts have been consciously silent, rendering only a few opinions construing the NFMA.... The judicial distance from the NFMA is about to an end.... Many, perhaps most, of the land management plans will be challenged in administrative appeals and litigation.

Beyond such overt interactions, the legal subsystem influences planning in more subtle ways—through fear. Fear of litigation on the part of the Forest Service leads to a lack of creativity and innovation, perpetuates and compounds unnecessary conservatism, and often exacerbates conflict rather than serving the opposite, desired purpose. Perhaps due to its less than stellar track record in court (for example, RARE II), the Forest Service has a loser's mentality and rushes to acquiesce to prevent future confrontation. The proposed Clearwater Plan illustrates these fear-induced planning problems.

The 1.8-million-acre Clearwater National Forest is surrounded by timber-dependent communities, has a complex physical-biological system, and two-thirds of the land base is minimally affected by development. Environmental groups routinely appeal timber sales and have targeted the forest for large wilderness withdrawals and NFMA legal action.

Forest planners are feeling the heat, and it shows in the draft plan. Three examples of planning problems arising from fear of the legal "boogeyman" follow.

Overestimation of Management Effects

The Draft Plan and DEIS fail to analyze the overestimation of management's effects on fisheries inherent in the forest's sediment and fisheries models. The models are based on a long series of consecutively dependent predictions of cause and effect and, in many cases, are based on limited data. Resulting error in any of these individual predictive relationships compounds, resulting in cumulative error. In the interest of "playing it safe," crucial relationships in the chain are based on conservative interpretation of data, conservative interpretation of physical-biological processes, and conservative assumptions. The result is inflated estimates of impacts and model-created conflict among resources. The practical result is a high degree of water quality and fisheries protection provided at the unnecessary expense of timber resources.

Unnecessary "Spreading of Impacts"

One district on the Clearwater Forest, intermingled with agricultural and private forest lands, is characterized by easily operable, productive timber sites, as well as a fishery resource and geology that vary greatly from other parts of the forest. The district has been intensively managed for timber for decades, yet the draft calls for a dramatic drop in timber harvest and most costly logging system. Based on model predictions, the forest's arbitrary goal for fisheries—based on a species that is not present in the area—will not be met without restricting harvest. In its rush to demonstrate "high quality" and protect itself from charges of inadequate resource protection, the forest actually increases its vulnerability to legal action by spreading the harvest into currently unroaded areas to compensate for reductions in the developed district.

Building a Cadillac When a Ford Will Do

A third example of problems arising from the fear of litigation is the Clearwater's propensity for highly engineered roads. Costly engineering (averaging $30,000 per mile on the Clearwater in 1985) is based on the wrong-headed rationale that an engineered road is synonymous with full mitigation. That assumption is pure bosh in my opinion.

A more creative—and realistic—approach to forest road building is the "minimum impact economic road" (MIER) (McGreer, 1986). As compared to an "engineered road," the MIER is designed and constructed to be narrower, to more closely fit the topography, and to have lower design speeds (resulting in far lower volumes of cut and fill and less disturbed soil area), yet have high levels of sediment control and mitigation. Economic roads constructed to strict environmental standards benefit timber, wildlife, and fisheries values when compared to the more conventional and traditional Forest Service standards.

Six years ago, Fairfax (1980) warned that in NFMA planning:

Wisdom, judgment, responsibility, creativity and initiative (could be) sacrificed to the least common denominator in hopes of achieving an accommodation which, if not in the public interest, is at least defensible should anyone decide to sue.

Her concern is borne out by the Clearwater Plan and other drafts, but I would argue that the lack of creativity and innovation in the interest of accommodation will boomerang, drawing more, not less, legal fire.

Caught in the Crossfire

The sociopolitical subsystem strongly interacts with the legal subsystem and has a major influence on the Forest Service planning performance. Arnold (1985) summarizes its influence this way:

The truth about forest management is this: it is no longer simply a technical and economic pursuit. Today it is social and political as well, replete with institutionalized citizen activism, an entrenched environmental bureaucracy and a coterie of lobbyists who would like to see the forest industry hogtied, if not butchered.

The sociopolitical system is driven more by values than by facts or science. At the polar ends of the controversy over forest land use are two dramatically different sets of values which view human interaction with the forest in divergent ways. On one end, humans are seen as having only negative impacts on the natural world. The forests can only be protected by taking humans, human commodity uses, and technology out of the picture; the best forest is one without people in it. The other value set places humans in the forest. It values productivity, profitability, and sustained yield; advocates the use of technology to achieve these goals; and sees humans as being in partnership with the forest.

If you are the forest supervisor of the Clearwater Forest, these value sets translate into relentless pressure by environmental groups to reduce and restrict commodity outputs on the one hand and, on the other, a local town "crisis rally" taking the national forest to task for not showing greater concern for local school support, employment, and community stability.[3]

This highly charged atmosphere is typical of the sociopolitical system surrounding the planning process. The draft plans are worse for the wear. They show definite signs of the agency's struggle to mitigate the pressure.

The plans perpetuate rather than resolve conflicts. Efforts to classify the forests into resource emphasis zones end up looking like dualistic, didactic pairs—black or white, no development or full development, with little or no range of grays (let alone technicolor!) in between.

The Draft Clearwater Plan contains basically three kinds of management prescriptions applied to large zones: (1) timber emphasis, (2) elk-fisheries emphasis with some timber harvesting, and (3) roadless-wilderness. Within these allocations, the plan misses countless opportunities to resolve problems. For example, the forest could have assumed lower open road densities to increase elk habitat potential in timber emphasis areas, and still harvest the same volume. Aggressive road closure programs in both timber and combined emphasis areas, along with economic road systems, could be used to limit impacts and improve timber availability at the same time. The plan could also address opportunities to cooperatively manage elk herds that make use of both public and private lands.

Planners did not look at opportunities for creative scheduling of management emphasis which recognizes the physical-biological and temporal dynamics of the forest. Why not, for example, try harvests with low-impact roads, followed by area closures on a long rotation to provide semi-primitive recreation areas and improved big game habitat?

A corollary to the either/or static view of management is the notion that humans can only have permanent negative effect on the environment, and the only way to "protect" noncommodity resources is to abandon management completely.

The plans are based on "strawmen" alternatives and a precon-

strained decision space. Alternatives that emphasize conflict (for example, "high timber outputs, no new wilderness") rather than seek "harmonious" management of the various resources and purportedly "represent" the position of one group or another are obviously not meant to fly. They are only meant to convince the various publics that an adequate range of alternatives was examined. There were no serious attempts on the Clearwater, for example, to meet both RPA timber goals and other resource targets. That kind of harmony was assumed simply to be impossible. The actual "decision space" occupies only a small portion of the range displayed in the plans, and is predetermined by the planning team's idea of what it can sell to the public.

With limited exceptions, public involvement has amounted to formalized nose counting and conflict avoidance. Typically, public meetings to discuss the draft plans were advertised as "open houses" so people could "provide comment." The Forest Service did not take the opportunity to improve its credibility by explaining the rationale behind the decision to choose a planned direction or to vigorously defend its position.

Hall (1986) urges the Forest Service to "be up front with the public" instead of hiding behind obscure analyses and legal interpretations. The forest plans will create winners and losers. The public involvement process should include being straight with both; "the losers deserve to know why, and how much, they lost."

While the plans describe in tedious detail the impacts of human activity on fish, wildlife, and water quality *ad nauseam,* they give short shrift to the human costs of management actions. The plans speak only in terms of "base employment" and "job distribution" and say nothing about unemployment in real human terms.

A case study (OWFT, 1985) of a national forest area in Oregon during the recent recession documents significant increases in treatment for depression, incidents of domestic violence, and demands for counseling in the schools in the face of shrinking financial support for schools and community services and loss of family income. Tharp (1985) makes similar observations. In one western Oregon community, property crime increased 40 percent in 18 months, and domestic violence increased over the same high unemployment period.

In the Forest Service political arena, local voices often lose out to the louder "national issues" despite congressional mandates to support local communities in recognition of the huge potential tax base tied up in federal land holdings in the West. Residents of dependent communities have—and are continuing to be asked to—set aside their productive resource base. Ignoring the full costs of giving up timber harvests and asking people to seek economic salvation in tourism (when most tourism jobs provide near poverty incomes) is a slap in the face.

These local losers at least deserve straight information about the future they should expect.

The Technical Subsystem

The Systems Age is characterized by information and communications technology, the increased importance of "abstract" work over manual work, the view of humans as resources with further potential and complementary to, rather than extensions of, machines (Ackoff, 1972; ISDC, 1984).

In terms of technology, forest planning is a very tall (if not impossible) order. The sheer volume of data and the complexity and dynamic nature of the resources, laws, and social demands force the Forest Service to rely heavily on computers. It is doubtful that the quality of the data base, the modeling assumptions and relationships, and/or the computer technology itself are necessarily up to the demands of the task. Forest planning technology is also redefining the role of the public, and the authority and control within the Forest Service.

FORPLAN, a linear programming optimization model aimed at finding the "best" alternative, is the agency's choice for NFMA planning. FORPLAN requires as inputs predictions about future conditions and then uses these in a deterministic way to calculate future outputs. Garcia (1985) points out that while FORPLAN may be the best technology available in the short run, the agency is trying to do a systems task with the wrong kind of model: "The National Forests exist for timber, grazing, watershed, wildlife and recreation. Each of these requires stochastic modeling, and all as one integrated system as well." She argues that what is needed is not a deterministic simulation but a dynamic one which includes random variables and where properties change over time. Even if we accept FORPLAN as the best hope for the present round of planning, there are problems with the way it is used.

The quality of the data base varies dramatically by resource, often far behind the demands of FORPLAN and the law. For example, forests tend to have a fairly sophisticated growth model for the timber resource, but strictly back-of-the-envelope estimates of the effects of various management prescriptions on recreation opportunities.

What cannot be modeled is as important as what can. To run FORPLAN at a reasonable cost, the size of the problem, that is, the number of planning unit-management prescriptions combinations assumed, must be limited. At best, small units of the forest must be aggregated into larger units and the inventory data averaged for modeling. Depending on the size and quality of the aggregations, the model may or may not resemble the "real world."

Size limitations, as well as model structure, eliminate opportunities to look at sequential changes in management emphasis—a key to the compatibility issue. A timber area can go from unroaded to harvested, but assuming that area access is then closed off, there is no way to model its reversion to a semi-primitive state. Thus, the model helps create conflict that need not exist in the real world.

Lack of an on-the-ground geographic link leads to implementation problems. For example, one may not actually harvest the areas as scheduled in the plan due to limitations on clear-cutting next to an existing opening in the forest canopy.

The emphasis on data and modeling alters the role of judgment. Computer output is used as gospel. It is held out as an "objective" shield against criticism and accountability, ignoring the fact that every relationship in the model is influenced by the values of the planners. The computer output, no matter how bad the input, is seductive; the process—"while projecting the impression of certainty—is plagued by the familiar 'garbage in, garbage out' problem" (Fairfax, 1980).

Computer technology also thwarts public participation. Many people cannot evaluate computers and do not understand complex technology. It is likely the concerned citizen will go away feeling frustrated, confused, and angry.

Planning technology is also elevating the role and power of the technical expert in at least two ways. First, by influencing which resources are emphasized. Take a forest, give it a large staff of landscape architects and the latest computerized system for analyzing "view-sheds," and it's no surprise that the plan emphasizes visual resources. A neighboring forest with a limited staff may not even have view zones mapped. Second, in a technology-dependent planning system, information and technical know-how are power. The importance and authority of the data processors and other technical experts are raised at the expense of the district manager's know-how.

A final concern associated with technology is with its cost. The Forest Service is sinking enormous amounts of money and staff time into the process, while seeming to spin its wheels. If critics want to point a finger at the cost of federal timber sales, they can start by looking at the overhead charges and time drain associated with planning activities.

The Agency Subsystem

The Forest Service is its own social subsystem and political animal. The agency has a tall hierarchical structure with line and staff personnel at multiple organizational levels. The way the agency operates affects—and is being affected by—NFMA planning.

Competent people are leaving the national forests. While I have no study to back up this statement, it is supported by industrywide observations and discussions with Forest Service personnel.

Fairfax (1980) speculated about changes in the agency, predicting among other things that the RPA/NFMA process would cause (1) a shift in hiring priorities, professional composition, and power and (2) increased centralization of decision making, politicizing the land-use planning process. These predictions have proven to be true, if local forests are representative, and may help explain why people are leaving the agency.

The Forest Service came into the 1960s and 1970s as a conservation leader. But it entered the 1980s licking its wounds, compliance-oriented, and prepared to bow to pressures rather than enhance its discretionary or advocacy values. Until very recent years, the agency had, what Fairfax calls "the good old Forest Service hubba hubba" which includes a cohesive structure, loyalty to the agency, and a "near-messianic sense of mission" (Fairfax, 1980). Agency personnel tended to see themselves and their decision making as "professional" and "apolitical." The judgment of on-the-ground managers was valued and power relatively decentralized.

The employee who joins the "hubba hubba" agency now finds himself in an alien land. One of the risks of RPA/NFMA is that it changes the initiative of the local forest from managing the land to managing the process. To effectuate the process, the forest places not only dollars but power in the hands of the "forest planners"—economists, systems analysts, and resource specialists. Many district personnel never see the plan until the public does, at which point they are stuck with implementing a plan in which they feel no ownership. The real loss is in plan quality which could benefit from the people who have "personal contact with the land, and who have lived long enough to have some pet theories and enthusiasms" (Fairfax, 1980).

Process emphasis requires that the agency not only hire people with particular skills, but often with personal agendas. Planning specialists for noncommodity resources come trained and prepared to be advocates for their disciplines. Add this dimension to the legal and political subsystems, and the role of the local decision maker changes. It is increasingly difficult for the forest supervisor to act other than as the team advises. What the planning staff thinks best may well have been negotiated with outside public interest groups. The temptation is not to make tough decisions or take risks, but to look for the road of least resistance and minimum political hassle.

The character of the organization is also being affected by sheer exhaustion. Some team members have been working on plans since 1979 with no final product to show for the years invested. Planning burnout will be an ongoing problem and will chase away good people.

CONCLUSIONS AND RECOMMENDATIONS

Sam Rayburn once observed that "Any jackass can kick down a barn, but it takes a skilled carpenter to build one." The role of planning critic comes much easier than craftsmanship. NFMA planning may be impossible to do. The process may become so entangled in legal challenges, public uproar, and technical impossibilities that it will collapse. This could well happen where the public controversies and stakes are the greatest: the highly productive, resource-rich far West. The unanswerable questions are, "Then what? Back to Congress?"

Assuming that the process continues to lumber along and assuming further the absence of any major advances in planning technology, I believe there are ways to improve the process and the plans in the near term.

The Forest Service could start by not acting like a Milquetoast. The fact is we live in an adversarial system of politics and justice, and the Forest Service cannot be everybody's buddy. The Forest Service should view appeals and litigation as part of the process and be prepared. The law is full of ambiguities. The agency should be up-front about its values and defend its own interpretation and discretion, not run from the fight to the false safety of accommodations and "objective" answers. Most forests have little or no direct contact with legal advice or feedback until it is too late. The resulting ignorance breeds fear and unnecessary soft underbellies in the plans.

The agency should encourage nontraditional thinking outside the bounds of conventional wisdom. The Forest Service is largely stuck in Machine Age thinking. Experience is a place to start, but it does not necessarily provide the innovative solution needed. One of the key roles of public involvement may be to provide an infusion of creative thinking into the process. For example, in Idaho a series of discussions between the timber industry and the Idaho Department of Fish and Game to seek out areas of agreement and joint recommendations to the Forest Service has been completed on several forests. The discussions have resulted in thoughtful joint proposals to compatibly manage for timber, fisheries, wildlife, and recreation.

Notably, the industry-fish and game discussions have occurred outside the formal public involvement program. The Forest Service was purposely excluded. Where parties see mutual value in reaching consensus, the process will work on its own. I doubt the Forest Service is particularly well served or learns very much from its own attempts at consensus-building workshops where there is no motivation for participants to develop consensus.

Systems Age success depends on a systematic view of the world and experimentation, whether one is bumping up against the courts, politics, or looking at the physical and biological system of a forest. Unless the Forest Service tries some experimental ventures into multiple-use management, the agency will never develop public trust in its ability to do better than in the past. Monitoring coupled with experimentation provides a workable package for building a more convincing track record in the future and responding to changing conditions.

Multiple use may seem to be a rusty concept, but the old dog still has a few tricks up its sleeve. One of the important messages in the MUSY Act is that forest planners should shoot for "harmonious" and "coordinated" management. Emphasizing conflicts plays into the hands of those who would tear the forests and the Forest Service apart.

Obviously, there will remain certain mutually exclusive activities and forest outputs. Optimizing for the whole implies sub-optimizing for the parts, but to date, the planning process is severely short-changing the opportunities for compatibility while busily feeding the fires of controversy.

Looking for harmony—for synthesis instead of simple addition—requires that humans remain in the forest picture. It depends on ingenuity and assumes there are positive human effects to be had. A planning process and future that deprive people of the responsibilities and opportunities to find creative solutions to environmental problems and to be productive citizens are surely as undesirable a legacy for our nation as a future without wilderness.

The Forest Service is not in an enviable situation. Whether the agency can perform in the turbulence of changing obligations, pressures, shrinking budgets, and mixed signals will depend on its ability to adapt, not acquiesce, and to be flexible, not weak.

NOTES

1. For example, the Wilderness Act (1964), Historic Preservation Act (1966), Wild and Scenic Rivers Act (1968), Endangered Species Act (1972), etc.
2. Ibid.
3. In August 1985, the town of Orofino, Idaho, was closed for a day to demonstrate the plight of the local community faced with the prospect of 40 percent unemployment as a result of timber industry layoffs and long-term uncertainties about timber supply.

BIBLIOGRAPHY

Ackoff, Russell. 1972. "The Second Industrial Revolution." In International Sociotechnical Design Consortium. *Performance by Design*. South Bend, IN: TSO.

Arnold, Ron. 1985. *The Environmental Battle*. Bellevue, WA: Free Enterprise Press.

Fairfax, Sally. 1980. "RPA and the Forest Service." In *A Citizens Guide to the Resource Planning Act and Forest Service Planning*. Washington, D.C.: The Conservation Foundation.

Garcia, Marcia. 1985. *FORPLAN and Land Management Planning*. Paper presented at the Symposium on Use of Systems Analysis in Forest Management, Athens, GA.

Hall, John. 1986. "Public Timber, Public Questions: NFPA Looks at 1986." *NFPA Special Report* (unnumbered).

McGreer, Dale. 1986. Interview with author. Potlatch Corporation, Lewiston, ID.

Oregon Women for Timber (OWFT). 1985. *A Case Study in Forest Planning: The Siuslaw National Forest*. Unpublished manuscript, Potlatch Corp., Western Division Wood Products, Forestry Library, Lewiston, ID.

Tharp, Mike. 1985. "Eugene, Oregon, May Be a Great Place to Live, But not Without a Job." *Wall Street Journal*, June 5, pp. 1, 17.

Trist, Eric. 1981. *The Evolution of Sociotechnical Systems: A Conceptual Framework and an Action Research Program*. Ontario Ministry of Labor, Ontario Quality of Working Life Center, Occasional Paper No. 2.

U.S. Forest Service. 1985. *Proposed Plan and Draft Environmental Impact Statement for the Clearwater National Forest*. Bremerton, WA: J & J Printing.

U.S. Forest Service. 1984. *Report of the Forest Service Fiscal Year 1984*. Washington, D.C.: U.S. Government Printing Office.

Wilkinson, Charles, and H. Michael Anderson. 1985. "Land and Resource Planning in the National Forest." *Oregon Law Review*, vol. 62, no. 1, p. 2.

Zivnuska, John A. 1980. *National Forest Planning in California for the 1980's*. Paper presented at the Annual Meeting of the Western Timber Association.

6

POLICY RESTRAINTS AND TRADE-OFFS IN AN URBAN NATIONAL RECREATIONAL AREA

John T. Tanacredi

ABSTRACT

Gateway National Recreation Area—26,645 acres of ocean beach, estuary, grasslands, forests and wildlife preserves in the New York-New Jersey area—is part of a program intended to bring the National Park System closer to the urban areas of the United States. The lands and waters now included in Gateway represent some of the last remnants of the original Hudson-Raritan estuarine system and are subject to delicate management decisions regarding the protection, preservation, and enhancement of these natural resources. Management at Gateway must strike a balance between resources and the park's stated mission to provide recreation. The trade-offs are defined by spatial and public-access limitations on the use of Gateway as a "recreation area." The resource management approach also depends on the particular recreation activity being considered as well as public expectations about what Gateway's multiple-use focus should be. This chapter discusses some of the natural resources management approaches to the "protection" and "use-by-reservation" zones and emphasizes those natural resources management activities and needs that aid in increasing or

John T. Tanacredi has been Natural Resource Management Specialist for the National Park Service at Gateway National Recreation Area since 1980 and is responsible for the coordination of research, natural resource management, and environmental compliance activities throughout the park. The author's comments are his own and do not necessarily reflect the position or policy of the U.S. Department of the Interior, National Park Service, or Gateway National Recreation Area.

maintaining desired levels of biological diversity in this unit of the U.S. National Park System.

Key Words: recreation, multiple-use, urban park, restoration ecology, urban wildlife refuge, Jamaica Bay, National Park Service, ecosystem revitalization, natural resources management

INTRODUCTION

The United States National Park Service has a unique opportunity in the new urban park units to reverse and, in many instances, restore or revitalize those natural and cultural systems which have been degraded or stressed by the urban environment. However, the Park Service must do more than just bring the national park ideals out of the "countryside" into the urban milieu. It must additionally be actively pursuing opportunities to demonstrate that abused natural resources can be regenerated, building a receptivity to man and the environment. The late René Dubos put it very well "To help . . . urban people move progressively and with increasing understanding from the completely humanized world into the wilderness" (Mitchell, 1978).

Recreation is a broad category encompassing a variety of passive and active activities, and is one of the largest and fastest growing economic forces in the United States. Since fishing and wildlife observation are totally dependent upon the natural flora and fauna of the park's ecosystem, recreational activities will compete with the use of these areas for wildlife preservation or industrial development. Pollution, for example, stemming from industrial and municipal waste disposal, will seriously limit or preclude certain recreational uses. However, even with these severe environmental stresses, Gateway's barrier beaches, estuarine ecosystem, upland forest, grasslands, and bay provide an experience with a natural coastal system to over 9 million visitors each year.

The park has been allocated into six management zones, each of which has specific planned management strategies and types of allowable use and development. The six zones are: (1) protection, (2) use-by-reservation, (3) beach, (4) unstructured recreation, (5) structured recreation, and (6) development.

This chapter will discuss some of the natural resources management approaches to the "protection" and "use-by-reservation" zones since it has been demonstrated that, in these zones, ecosystems are more sensitive to human activities and are not suitable in the sense of (resource consumptive) "active" recreation. Since these two areas encompass the majority of the park's acreage, management cannot just provide "recreational spaces" but rather, as the Second World Conference on

National Parks in 1972 endorsed, must work toward shaping Gateway to be a place "where visitors are allowed to enter, under special conditions, for inspirational, educative and recreative purposes" (Wauer, 1982).

This discussion will highlight the significance of these special areas in an urban context as well as emphasize those natural resources management activities and needs that will aid in increasing or maintaining desired levels of biological diversity in this unit of the U.S. National Park System.

QUALITY OF THE RESOURCE

Due in part to the impacts associated with its proximity to a major metropolitan system, and in part to the National Park Service's inheriting already impaired natural resources, conserving the scenery at Gateway National Recreation Area in some cases may require manipulating these highly altered systems, and then allowing nature to take its course. The basic premise to such activities is to mimic natural conditions by providing an atmosphere conducive to increasing habitat diversity and for increasing levels of species diversity approaching historical levels.

The U.S. Department of Interior's management policies of 1975 have recognized the need to determine the attributes and constraints of all land within the park system and to classify the resources accordingly. Management objectives have been developed by land class and are applied to all units regardless of their administrative designation, that is, natural, historical, or recreation park (Stottlemyer, 1981).

Open spaces are urgently needed in the United States, particularly near metropolitan areas. Recreation areas such as Gateway, while created for use by the general public, were also envisioned to be free from exploitative practices for the protection of wildlife and their habitat. It was noted recently that some of Gateway's natural resources "... do not clearly bespeak 'quality' much less national distinctiveness. To create quality here will require more dollars and more consensus than have been available so far. One target would be cleaning up Jamaica Bay" (Cahn, 1982).

The question presented here is: How much of the resource should be manipulated to some level of environmental quality? There are clearly areas which, by allowing nature to take its course, would revitalize themselves to almost original levels of quality. A related question becomes one of sheer quantity: How much area is left to "nonuse"? Perhaps the most important example in this regard is the condition of Jamaica Bay. Continued pollution loads limit the diversity and numbers of organisms in the bay. If the pollution can be prevented, however, natural processes could certainly return the natural systems to an historically higher level of "quality."

This reflects René Dubos's belief that " ... an ecosystem that has been changed can be brought back to a good condition if you help nature to function with the natural repair systems that exist" (Dubos, 1978). The bay, in addition to its ecological significance, therefore provides for urban dwellers the "spirit of individual place" René Dubos spoke of (Dubos, 1980).

Diversity

In a major population area such as New York City, where there is urban encroachment upon the few remnant natural areas that exist, fostering habitat preservation and enhancement becomes almost a monumental task. Those areas that have been despoiled by such human activities as landfilling are still subject to natural processes and are forever subject to a myriad of "development" scenarios. Previously filled lands are not "natural," the argument goes, so that "preservation" of the overlaying developing natural system—no matter how diverse or close to the primitive habitat type—is best forgone or, at the minimum, prime for resource-consumptive activities. Perhaps more importantly, the zeal to develop this type of habitat is expressed in such understated terms that, not until one observes the small encroachments added up over a long period of time, does one observe the loss. Likened to an ecological triage, management in response to user-demands must utilize the more "devastated" area first. This devastated area is highly subjective, and is usually measured by the area's level of accumulated knowledge or data (that is, plant species composition or occasional use by waterfowl, etc.) or by a desire not to utilize another area so that these "less desirable" spaces can be developed.

At Floyd Bennett Field, for example, from purely an ecological standpoint, management is plagued by the conflict and competition over the multi-use capacity concept of the area. Identifying Floyd Bennett Field as a "refuge" along the Atlantic Flyway becomes more a function of visitor-use than environmental reality since it functions unabated as a refuge even in its present condition.

In urban areas, it has been taken for granted that species inventories would be easy to develop since urban systems are composed of less a diversity of plant and animal life. Yet some recent evidence has exhibited the ecological resilience of ecosystems in urban areas (Venezia and Tanacredi, 1982).

High diversity is of importance to scientists and urban natural resources managers since the potential carrying capacity of a system to support a high diversity of wildlife will be significant to visitor experiences as well as the particular ecosystem's stability. Greater habitat diversity will increase the biological carrying capacity of a system, yet greater diversity will not directly increase visitor carrying capacities for an area unless a particular vegetation is so unique—as in an arboretum—that visitors would be attracted to this area of the park just to be able to afford the experience. In order to increase visitor numbers, if this is a primary premise we go by, there must be a reduction of habitat diversity by keeping areas in "manageable" parcels so that these areas will be able to handle a greater variety of "recreational activities" of greater numbers. When the type of recreational activity is directed away from protection and preservation, then natural carrying capacities will be reduced. The expense is the loss of contiguous natural areas. Ultimately, because of these breaks in the overall parcel of open space available for use, there is a consummate reduction in natural habitat, biological carrying capacities, and, in most instances, overall species diversity. As Dr. Dubos has pointed out, "From the point of view of human and environmental quality, it is probable that diversity and flexibility are more valuable than productivity and efficiency" (Dubos, 1978).

Natural Resource Base

The term "urban wildlife" is utilized to describe those species that have adapted to urban encroachments, and are somehow removed from their "wild" kin. Without detracting from the fact that management of such organisms may in some instance require somewhat manipulated technologies in the urban setting, traditional wildlife management techniques should continue to be applied. One very significant difference— but only in gradation, not in content—is the need for greater emphasis on effective educational programs evolving from our focus on the natural resource base. Maintaining natural sites near metropolitan areas facilitates environmental education as well as provides for park managers an understanding that the research function and the parks' role in local decision making can create public support for conservation programs both within and without urban areas (MacMullen, 1968).

What the resource manager becomes, therefore, has been described as being "... the translator of scientific material into the language of the decision-makers. He must see that the research meets the needs of the decision-maker and that the decision-maker has the scientific data necessary to make reasonable decisions ... " when deciding on the use or nonuse of a park's natural resources (Dolan, Hayden, and Soucie, 1978).

As R. H. Wauer has put it: "Today there is a growing acceptance of the fact that ignorance of science, like ignorance of the law, is an unjustifiable excuse for environmental abuse" (Wauer, 1980). Trial and error does not work when it comes to the National Park Service's primary responsibility of protecting the resource for future generations.

One of the primary roles of the urban park was to provide a National Park Service experience. At Gateway there is also the added opportunity to remind the city dwellers that there is a larger "nature" outside the city, and one should be aware of it and if possible explore it. J. L. Sax notes: "The growth of the National Park System is justified by a recognition that the symbolism of parks needs to be brought closer to the public, not that the symbol should be urbanized" (Sax, 1980).

When the urban public thinks of or is questioned about Gateway's wildlife, invariably one or two living species are recognizable to them: Norway rats, insects, and Phragmites—possibly fish—but generally little else. Ideally, inventory is the first step in determining a natural resource base and the suitability for a variety of potential uses or non-use.

For example, some original vegetation work conducted at the Jamaica Bay Wildlife Refuge in 1976 identified some 65 or so families of plants (Bridges, 1976). This basic list was mapped on vegetative maps and subsequently used as "planning" maps. The survey techniques included aerial photograph review and limited field verifications. Due to time constraints, little transect work was accomplished. During the summer of 1982, a detailed floral inventory covering only 10 acres of some 100 acres in the northern section of Floyd Bennett Field was conducted. A total of 350 species comprising over 85 families were identified for the parkwide herbarium reference files (Venezia and Tanacredi, 1982). What is acknowledged here is that the level of detail and scope of work committed to species composition revealed an even greater plant species number than previously thought. The implication for management is that activities requiring major manipulations of the existing landscape may not be tenable based on already existing plant diversity level knowledge.

Biological Productivity and Natural Function

In unstressed ecosystems it may be relatively easier to demonstrate the economic value of the system; for example, several investigations regarding economic analyses on wetlands have been conducted exhibiting the significance of these ecotypes (Thibodeau and Ostro, 1981). Yet, even in stressed estuarine wetlands, their ability to continue to function naturally and provide relatively high biological productivity levels is significant. Once an ecosystem is lost due to filling, development, etc., its potential use in the form of biological productivity, based upon its natural functioning, may become irreversible. Remnant parcels must be allowed to function unimpaired and be reinitiated into the landscape of the original habitat types and forms, if the overall ecosystem is to have a chance to regenerate to some predetermined historical level.

In order to accomplish this, efficient management of renewable natural resources must depend on a knowledge of the interrelations of organisms of various levels of activity and their relationships to abiotic subsystems. This interdependence of various strata of organisms with the same habitat and their relationship to the environment is well documented (Odum, 1971). Manipulation of components must, therefore, be carefully in tune with the functioning of the system as a whole before management decisions are implemented.

Most work on terrestrial systems, for example, will be limited to the relationship of the dominant plant species or vegetation with its consumer. *Phragmites communis* has long been thought not only to be the dominant plant species at Gateway but also to be of little wildlife support significance. Both of these points have been shown to be somewhat inappropriate. Depending on where you are in the park, *Phragmites* may very well be the dominant cover species. However, their frequency and abundance levels are about twenty-third in the park. In addition, recent studies have shown *Phragmites* to contribute as much, if not more, organic material to detrital accumulations in estuarine sytems as does *Spartina alterniflora*. *Phragmites* also provide excellent escape habitat for pheasant, meadow voles, etc., while acting to prepare soils for the introduction of other plant species (U.S. Fish and Wildlife Service, 1980).

Preservation of the natural functioning of ecosystems has been a prime resource management goal of each national park. In 1963, the Leopold Committee, an advisory board to Interior Secretary Udall, recommended that natural processes such as fire, insect outbreaks, coastal geomorphologic phenomena, and the like be allowed to operate "with reasonable freedom" within the national parks. "Reasonable freedom" generally means freely within an ecosystem so long as (1) no species or biotic community is exposed to the possibility of extinction, (2) no unacceptable losses to other resources are anticipated, and (3) there is no threat to human safety (Bonnicksen and Stone, 1982).

It has been Park Service policy to restore to its natural condition ecosystems that have undergone major European-settler-induced changes. How closely the natural condition is approximated depends upon existing knowledge of that condition and to what degree the biological and physical processes molding that system presently can simulate or regenerate presettlement conditions. For example, at Floyd Bennett Field, vegetated areas have been allowed to function unimpeded for a minimum of 15 to 20 years. The diversity of plant material has been shown to be good. Once a detailed inventory of all plants is made for the field, the natural resources management option could be to leave these developing systems alone. Regardless of the decision or lack of decision, vegetative succession will continue. To return Floyd Bennett Field to Barren Island—a part of the coastal outwash plain and a marsh island in Jamaica Bay—is impractical. Allowing natural marsh accretion along Floyd Bennett Field's periphery and planting indigenous species propagated from existing plants or their seeds from the area are examples of providing for natural functioning of ecosystems to regenerate and revitalize themselves. Care must be taken, however, to preserve intact natural systems and not to allow, in the case of marsh restoration, a substitution for natural systems by man-recreated systems.

For example, it has been demonstrated that the benefit-cost ratio of preservation of the Charles River wetlands near Boston, Massachusetts, is 150:1 based upon a conservatively determined worth of $150,000 per acre if left undeveloped (Thibodeau and Ostro, 1981). Their market value for construction is between $200 and $5,000 per acre. This ratio was projected as being a typical benefit-cost ratio for wetland preservation efforts near urban areas. Under the mitigative measures called for in environmental compliance procedures for U.S. Army Corps of Engineers projects, recreated marshes are viable substitutes for filling, ditching, and otherwise eliminating natural marsh areas. Such replacement marshes have been shown to be of lower quality and biological productivity than natural coastal marshes (Seluk-Race and Christie, 1982). In some cases where marshes are planted to reduce shoreline erosion, or in cases where degraded tidal wetlands are replanted to be influenced again by tidal action, this technique has proven effective. A two-acre area at the Jamaica Bay Wildlife Refuge threatened by erosion was replanted and has stabilized the shore. The bottom line, however, must be the maintenance of natural functioning ecosystems with a commensurate reduction in pollutional loads so as to allow the recruitment and increase of natural biological productivity and diversity levels. The value of natural ecosystems from ecological and economic standpoints has been well documented (Hall and Day, 1977; Farnworth et al., 1981).

Multi-Use Capacity

Floyd Bennett Field, which is planned for a variety of recreational uses on a macro-scale level, is an area that requires micro-scale assessments in order to determine carrying capacities for wildlife. Variety in habitat components is essential for food, shelter, and visitor perceptions of wildlife. Planning wildlife habitat must be multidisciplinary in approach, and this includes the realization that man is a biological component in the system under study.

Considering capacities of parcels of space within an overall unit poses problems that directly affect natural systems. For example, consideration of types of vegetation to support wildlife should include more than just food source, but rather suitable habitat. This involves escape cover, nesting space, alternative species (floral and faunal) interactions, continuity of habitat, and potential nuisance problems to and from man. Wildlife do not recognize boundary or jurisdictional lines. Few animals have small home ranges or territories in which they will remain. Contiguous systems, not potmarked sites within an entire district, must be maintained and monitored. As S. M. Gold has put it, we should be "... emphasizing the fact that we over-groom our parks when most portions of them could be left more natural to benefit wildlife and also save money. Once the economic value of attractive natural areas is established, then development pressures, which would predictably reverse positive aspects of environmental quality, would decrease precipitously" (Gold, 1973).

Traditionally, urban parks have emphasized lawn areas and areas that contain only mature trees. Yet, other area types are important; shrubs, saplings, and a tall herbaceous ground cover will be productive to a variety of wildlife. Grey and Deneke (1978) had noted the benefits of urban forests such as climate amelioration (temperature modification in cities which are generally 0.5 to 1.5 degrees Celsius warmer during the day than the countryside), wind protection, water runoff control, noise abatement, air pollution abatement, and aesthetics.

Fragmented ecosystems affect migratory species, many of which have been characteristically dependent upon large tracts of forested areas. Long-distant migrants decrease when large tracts of land are broken into smaller tracts and isolated from a source of repopulation. Floyd Bennett Field and Jamaica Bay Refuge are two of the remnant tracts and remaining coastal estuarine systems in New York that can support such a variety of species. Extirpated wildlife now find the 17,000-plus acres of Jamaica Bay their last outpost.

It has been shown that provision of freshwater habitat directly influences the variety of wildlife (Franklin, 1981). Several activities have been suggested which can improve habitat conditions in urban areas: (1) maintaining wetland habitat, (2) creating additional impoundments where practical, (3) erecting various types of nesting boxes, and (4) providing brush (cut for road and trail maintenance) near woodland borders as valuable habitat for species ranging from bacterial decomposers to fungi, wood-boring insects, amphibians, reptiles, birds, and mammals.

Without implementing long-term monitoring or carrying capacities in a multi-use area, the detection of alterations and their prime causes will be extremely difficult. Comprehensive monitoring programs covering habitat management activities must be in place prior to implementation of any planning scenarios (Gregg, 1980). Critical thresholds of visitor demands must be acknowledged prior to placing ecosystems under their stress. In urban areas where systems are presently in danger of being irreversibly lost or irreparably damaged, biological carrying capacities must be compatible with visitor demand levels so that natural regenerative capacities of systems can work unchecked to restore or maintain equilibrium conditions for that ecosystem. The abiotic component of natural systems never changes in function no matter what the political, social, economic, or even developmental conditions are.

Natural Resource Management Case Histories

Erosion, Shoreline Dynamics, and Marsh Restoration

Letting nature take its course is in concert with the conservation-preservation ethic of the National Park Service and, in many cases, is the most economical way to handle a particular ecological problem. However, application at Gateway has depended upon existing environmental conditions and the originally intended purpose of this "recreation area" (Leatherman, Godfrey, and Buckley, 1978; Psuty, Nordstrom, and Allen, 1976; Godfrey, 1978). Natural resources management considerations are sometimes dependent on man's manipulation of the landscape. An example is beach nourishment, where sand naturally accruing due to littoral drift is recycled back through the system to the eroding and high-visitor-use area (Niedoroda, Coch, and Godfrey, 1975). Thus, natural tasks would be performed that have previously been rendered unworkable.

Several sites at Gateway have been determined to be ideal for applying breakwater technology to control erosion. Plumb Beach, an area of only 15 acres yet under intensive visitor use, has been subject to severe erosion impacts. Several marsh restoration-revitalization projects have been implemented and are presently being monitored for long-term erosion prevention (Gay and Enrico, 1979). Once the natural system (replanting of *Spartina alterniflora*) has been able to propagate with help from man, nature can take its course to "develop" this marshland (Gay and Tanacredi, 1982). Coupling the breakwater and marsh restoration approaches will aid these environmentally stressed areas. Ignoring past mistakes which have altered the barrier and allowing the system to oscillate significantly is not appropriate where many factors must be considered, not the least of which is public access and usage of the seashore (Godfrey, 1975).

Water Quality Monitoring

In the mid–1960s, public health officials studying the problems of sewage sludge disposal in the New York Bight noted that bottom sediments offshore had higher populations of coliform bacteria. Marine biologists had been collecting information on the effects of sewage sludge, dredge spoils, and chemical wastes on living resources including plankton, bottom dwelling invertebrates, and finfish. Initial results back from sampling stations through the Bight apex indicated that waste materials were not accumulating in a single restricted area but rather were spreading out over much of the New York Bight apex (Pearce, 1976). During the summer of 1976, low dissolved oxygen levels in area coastal waters lasted from June through September. Millions of dollars worth of commercial shellfish were killed. Beaches were closed along Long Island and the Jersey shore.

In response to this pollution episode, Gateway has instituted monitoring of bacteriological water quality into its management activities. Weekly samples are currently being collected at some 28 sites within the waters of our jurisdictional boundaries. These samples provide us with bacteriological water quality data at existing beaches. Since bathing and beachcombing are among the primary uses of Gateway—and one of the most enjoyed activities by the American public—water quality plays a critical role in acceptability of its use (Heatwole and West, 1980).

Water pollution within the New York coastal region, and particularly within the harbor area, is well known to the public. Such conditions can and do affect the quality of the beach environment and often result in negative user perceptions of local beaches (David, 1971). Under the terms of the Federal Water Pollution Control Act, the New York harbor and estuary waters gradually are being cleaned up. While much work remains to be done (Tanacredi, 1977), for example, reduce waste hydrocarbon contributions, improvements are likely to continue to the extent that "closed areas" may become sites for aquatic contact-recreation type activities.

Landfill and Development

Considerable amounts of Gateway properties were created by previous landfill activities. Pennsylvania Avenue Landfill, for example, is a manmade peninsula of 110 acres located on the north shore of Jamaica Bay. Refuse was dumped from 1959 until 1962. Dried sewage sludge was deposited there from 1962 until 1972; and, from 1972 to 1985, construction debris was being placed so that contour lines of 75–100 feet above mean sea level exist. As part of a cooperative agreement, a plan developed in 1974 by the City of New York would be considered for implementation. The plan used various disciplines in coordinating the creation of a recreational facility out of construction fill—from raw fill to finished terraced park (NYC DOS Plan, 1974).

The implementation of the Pennsylvania Avenue Plan would be an attempt to echo nature, and designers had sought to create an environment that functioned both as a recreational facility and as natural habitat. Vistas, terraced landscapes, public access, and energy (methane gas) generation are all advantages assigned to this landfill scheme. The problems that have developed are basically hazardous material leachates into surrounding waters. As of 1981, it was found that upward of 30 million gallons of hazardous wastes—including PCB-contaminated waste oil—had been routinely, yet illegally, deposited at the two north shore landfills. The National Park Service will, in response to potential public health hazards, direct long-term research efforts toward determining to what extent these contaminants are entering the Jamaica Bay ecosystem as well as establishing a floral and faunal inventory to aid in the future reclamation of this land into the natural landscape.

CONCLUSION

Gateway has been noted as having a "significance of complexity," that is, the National Park Service is to provide here—or has the opportunity to provide here—a creative leap in leadership and stewardship to translate past military, abandoned, and remnant pieces of open space and stressed-degraded coastal ecosystems into traditional Park Service purposes and mandates. We must certainly recognize that this urban park is interrelated with the myriad of public lands that surround it, yet Gateway provides one of the last spaces for many species of wildlife—both floral and faunal—remaining in the metropolitan area. Management must, therefore, focus on this latter concern. As Devereaux Butcher noted, we must "keep (National Parks) free from artificial amusements, which have no rightful place in nature sanctuaries but defeat their purpose; and at all cost must prevent the deterioration of the National Park and Monument system to the common level of playgrounds and commercialized resorts . . . " (Butcher, 1969).

The majority of Americans believe as the 1980 public opinion on environmental issues report prepared by the Council on Environmental Quality stated:

All told if public opinion is any guide, it would seem that business continues to have little recourse but to learn to cope with the fact that environmental protection no longer is the exclusive domain of a handful of professional social critics and environmental activists, but the continuing concern of the public as a whole (CEQ, 1980).

The true test for Gateway is to reverse the trends of "hundreds of little decisions" that have added up over the span of years to a conscious loss of habitat which may never have been planned for (Odum, 1982). It is certainly easier and politically more feasible to make decisions on a single tract of land or a single issue than to attempt a policy or plan of land use on a large scale. I call this tyranny of small decisions "nickel-dime ecology." This is expedient decision making based upon the most paltry of ecological data or information.

Gateway, as well as the National Park Service in its urban context, cannot be short-changing ecological principles by anything less than a significant commitment to natural and cultural resource protection and management. What is occurring is that, even within other national park units, there are "islands of activities" surrounded by park boundaries which are not isolated from urban infringement. This insularization of activities cuts off the natural flow of species in an area; and, similar to the isolation phenomenon being identified in larger park units, there is an isolation of species with little natural recruitment within parks themselves. Man, in his traditional development and multi-use scenarios, simplifies ecosystems and reduces their diversity. Certain organisms are forced to move or adapt, or they die. The loss of some species endangers other species and so on until an entire ecosystem may be lost. Harwood has noted that, as " ... we reduce biotic diversity in more and more habitat, we at the same time create islands of remaining natural habitat" (Harwood, 1982). The smaller an isolated habitat becomes, the fewer species it contains. When we maintain monocultures of cut grass, for example, it represents an imposed sterility and a negative example of diversified land management.

In sum, the natural resources management approaches within this urban national park exhibit these significant restraints and trade-offs:

1. It is difficult to maintain multiple-use practices when respective uses are so close to one another. Management is therefore undermined by the conflict and competition over the multi-use capacity of an area.

2. Relatively unmodified or recuperating natural portions of the park must be closely guarded and maintained in as primitive a state as possible.

3. Visitor numbers increase; habitat diversity decreases since areas are kept in "manageable parcels" so as to handle overall greater types of recreational activities. At the expense of a loss of contiguous natural areas, large tracts of open space are parcelled out into activity zones to support greater visitor carrying capacities. Biological carrying capacities must determine visitor carrying capacities, not vice versa.

4. Extensive natural systems inventorying, establishing a detailed data base, must be accomplished early on in the planning of an urban park with an ongoing annual monitoring network established to note alterations imposed on systems

by types of recreational activity. This must be accomplished through traditional biological and natural resources management survey and inventory techniques. This should not be a planning activity.

5. There must be a closer tie between natural resources management and traditional National Park Service interpretive skills and programs in order to make scientific data more palatable to the general public as well as to managers.

6. Reduction of pollutional loads to estuarine-coastal ecosystems, coupled with allowing natural processes to run unabated, will return degraded natural systems to historically higher levels of productivity and aesthetic quality.

Bibliography

Bonnicksen, T. M., and E. C. Stone. 1982. "Managing Vegetation within U.S. National Parks, A Policy Analysis." *Journal of Environmental Management*, vol. 6, no. 2: 109–22.

Bridges, J. T. 1976. "Vegetation Survey, Soils Map and Estimate of Plant Health Conditions at the Jamaica Bay Wildlife Refuge," Contract #CX 1600–5–0010. National Park Service unpublished report.

Cahn, R. 1982. *Christian Science Monitor*, 14–18 June, series on national parks.

Council on Environmental Quality, Executive Office of the President. 1980. "Report on Public Opinion of Environmental Issues." Washington, D.C.: US GPO, p. 45.

David, E. L. 1971. "Public Perceptions of Water Quality." *Water Resources Research*, vol. 7, no. 3: 453.

Dolan, R., B. P. Hayden, and G. Soucie. 1978. "Environmental Dynamics and Resource Management in the U.S. National Parks." *Journal of Environmental Management*, vol. 2, no. 3: 249–58.

Dubos, R. 1980. *The Wooing of Earth*. New York: Charles Scribner and Sons.

———. 1978. "Think Globally, Act Locally—An Interview with Dr. Rene Dubos." *EPA Journal* reprint, October, no. 5.

Farnworth, E. G. et al. 1981. "The Value of Natural Ecosystems: An Economic and Ecological Framework." *Environmental Conservation*, vol. 8, no. 4: 275–82.

Franklin, T. M. 1981. "Wildlife in City Parks." *Trends in Urban Forestry*, vol. 18, no. 4: pp. 14–18.

Gay, B. L., and J. Enrico. 1979. "Transplanting the Valuable Marsh Grass *Spartina alterniflora* in an Environmentally Stressed Area." Proceedings Second Conference on Research National Parks, San Francisco, CA, p. B4.

Gay, B. L., and J. T. Tanacredi. 1982. "Shoreline Stabilization through Marsh Restoration." *Trends*, vol. 19, no. 4: 14–17.

Godfrey, P. J. 1978. "Management Guideline for Parks on Barrier Beaches." *Parks*, vol. 2, no. 4: 5–10.

———. 1975. Comments on Present Beach Management Philosophy in Relation to Gateway NRA. University of Massachusetts, NPS CRU Report 9, p. 9.

Gold, S. M. 1973. *Urban Recreation Planning*. New York: Academic Press. p. 333.

Gregg, W. P. 1980. "Development Alternative: New Directions." Barrier Island

Forum and Workshop Proceedings, Cape Cod National Seashore, May 1980, pp. 43–53.

Grey, G. W., and F. J. Deneke. 1978. *Urban Forestry*. New York: John Wiley and Sons, p. 279.

Hall, C. A. S., and John W. Day, Jr., eds. 1977. "Economic Values and Natural Ecosystems." In *Ecosystem Modeling in Theory and Practice*. New York: John Wiley and Sons, pp. 134–71.

Harwood, M. 1982. "Math of Extinction." *Audubon* 9: 19.

Heatwole, C. A., and N. C. West. 1980. "Beach Use and User Constraints in the NYC Coastal Region." New York State Sea Grant Report Series, NYSG-RS–80–01, p. 3.

Leatherman, S. P., P. J. Godfrey, and P. A. Buckley. 1978. "Management Strategies for National Seashores." Proceedings Symposium of Technical, Environmental, Socioeconomical and Regulatory Aspects of Coastal Zone Planning and Management, San Francisco, CA, 14–16 March, pp. 322–77.

Mitchell, J. G. 1878. "The Re-greening of Urban America." *Audubon* 15: 29–52.

New York City Department of Sanitation and U.S. Environmental Protection Agency. 1974. "From Landfill to Park." An Experiment in Construction Waste Management at the Pennsylvania Avenue Landfill Site, NYC Department Concept Plan 21–74, December, p. 80.

Niedoroda, A. W., N. Coch, and P. J. Godfrey. 1975. "Preliminary Report on Erosion Problems at Great Kills Park and Sandy Hook, Gateway NRA." University of Massachusetts, NPS CRU-Report #8, p. 11.

Odum, E. P. 1971. *Fundamentals of Ecology*. 3rd ed. Philadelphia: W. B. Saunders Press.

Odum, W. E. 1982. "Environmental Degradation and the Tyranny of Small Decision." *Bio Science*, vol. 32, no. 9.

Pearce, J. B. 1976. "Our Coastal Waters: An Endangered Zone." *The Science Teacher*, vol. 43, no. 9 (December).

Psuty, N., K. F. Nordstrom, and J. R. Allen. 1976. "Application of Coastal Geomorphology to Management of Beach Resources in Gateway NRA." National Park Service unpublished report, pp. 151–54.

Sax, Joseph L. 1980. "Mountains Without Handrails: Reflections on the National Parks." Ann Arbor: The University of Michigan Press, pp. 84–86.

Seluk-Race, M., and D. R. Christie. 1982. "Coastal Zone Development: Mitigation, Marsh Creation, and Decision Making." *Journal of Environmental Management*, vol. 6, no. 4, pp. 317–28.

Stottlemyer, J. R. 1981. "Evolution of Management Policy and Research in the National Parks." *Journal of Forestry* 79: 16–20.

Sudia, T. 1973. "Meeting Urban Wildlife Needs." In: *Man, Nature, City*. Proceedings NPS Urban Ecosystem Conference. Pub. #0–528–438.

Tanacredi, J. T. 1977. "Petroleum Hydrocarbons: Contribution to the Marine Environment." *Journal Water Pollution Control Federation* 2: 216.

Thibodeau, F. R., and B. D. Ostro. 1981. "An Economic Analysis of Wetland Protection." *Journal of Environmental Management* 12: 19–30.

U.S. Fish and Wildlife Service letter dated November 10, 1980, Ref: Masters

Thesis. "A Study of the Common Reed Grass, *Phragmites communis*, in the Coastal Zone of Delaware," 764 pages.

Venezia, K., and J. T. Tanacredi. 1982. "Terrestrial Vegetative Inventory." Gateway NRA, unpublished report.

Wauer, R. H. 1982. "A Perspective of Natural Resources Management in the National Park Service." Washington Offices of Resource Management, U.S. Department of the Interior, National Park Service.

———. 1980. "The Role of the National Park Service Natural Resources Manager." University of Washington/CPSU Report 8–80–2, p. 15.

7

A NEST-EGG APPROACH TO THE PUBLIC LANDS

Frank J. Popper

ABSTRACT

For more than half a century, America has lacked a clear, agreed upon national idea of what to do with the public lands. By now many of the ideas we use to manage the lands, including multiple use, have only local, legalistic, or bureaucratic scope. The contestants in today's public land debates are repeating preservation-versus-exploitation arguments that go back at least to the time of Theodore Roosevelt. This chapter examines the course of American public land policy since the late eighteenth century. It then suggests a different, more fruitful way for the nation to deal with its public lands, what the chapter calls a "nest-egg approach." This approach is also rooted in history, but is better suited to the conditions of late-twentieth-century America, I believe, than other approaches. In addition, it provides a practical way to revitalize the concept of multiple use.

Key Words: multiple use, public lands, national parks, national forests, Bureau of Land Management, James Watt, Sagebrush Rebellion.

REDISCOVERING THE FEDERAL LANDS

Before their deserved disappearance, James Watt and the Sagebrush Rebellion did the country a genuine service. They refocused public attention on a permanent issue of national development: the use and possible disposal of the vast federal lands in the West, rural-to-wilderness holdings that comprise 30 percent of the entire United States.

For most of American history, the public lands were a high priority national issue. Their uses determined the future of the American economy. Their disposal to settlers controlled the course of Western expansion. But in the 1890s, the Census Bureau and Frederick Jackson Turner declared the frontier statistically and economically closed. In 1934, the Taylor Grazing Act physically and legally closed it by abolishing homesteading, which had long been in steep decline. Then the public lands largely disappeared from the nation's agenda, except for occasional outbursts such as the Sagebrush Rebellion (Popper, 1984).

For more than half a century, America has lacked a clear, agreed-upon national idea of what to do with the public lands. For much of this period it has nearly forgotten about them. Federal agencies, state and local governments, environmentalists, and developers continue to spar over the lands. But most of the concepts they use to plan, manage, protect, sell, and buy them originated well before 1934, often in the early nineteenth century, and are distinctly showing their age. By now many of these ideas, including multiple use, have only local, legalistic, or bureaucratic meaning. They are no longer intended to shape the country's development on a Westwide regional scale, much less on a national one. The contestants in today's public land debates are repeating preservation-versus-exploitation arguments that go back at least to the time of Theodore Roosevelt. They are designing policies accordingly.

I would like to examine the course of American public land policy over the years and then suggest a different, more fruitful way for the nation to deal with its public lands, what I call a nest-egg approach. This approach is also rooted in history, but is better suited to the conditions of late twentieth-century America than its competitors. In addition, it provides a useful way to reinvigorate the concept of multiple use.

THE FEDERAL FIEF

One can still surprise an East or West Coast listener with the fact that the federal government owns nearly a third of the nation's land. The vast bulk is in the Intermountain West from the Sierra-Cascades to the Rockies, and in Alaska. Thus the state governments of Alaska, Idaho, Nevada, Oregon, and Utah lack formal jurisdiction over more than half their territory; Arizona, California, Colorado, New Mexico, and Wyoming over more than a third of theirs. The land is all but uninhabited. You could hike 1,800 miles, from central Oregon southeast to southern Nevada, then northeast to the midpoint of the Utah-Colorado border, and southeast again to southern New Mexico on the Mexican border. Aside from minor jumps—mostly across other public land—you would never leave the property of the Interior Department's Bureau of Land Management (BLM). It holds 44 percent of the land in states west of the Rockies.

You could take another 1,800-mile BLM hike from southeast California on the Mexican border to northeast Montana on the Canadian border. The California-Montana hike fittingly intersects the Oregon-New Mexico one in southern Utah, one of America's most forbidding places. You could take a 2,300-mile BLM hike around Alaska, from the southern Yukon Territory border northwest to near Barrow—the northernmost town in the United States, and then southwest to the Yukon River Delta and the middle of the Alaska Peninsula on the Bering Sea. The BLM hikes—call them branches of the James Watt Trail—would cross deserts, mountains, forests, plains, rivers, tundras, and ice. You would rarely encounter a settlement or even step on the property of the Agriculture Department's Forest Service, the second largest federal land agency (16 percent of the land in states west of the Rockies), or that of the Interior Department's Fish and Wildlife Service (8 percent), or its National Park Service (6 percent).

The public lands contain a prodigious share of America's resources. Forest Service land—mainly in Oregon, Washington, and northern California—produces 40 percent of the nation's marketable timber, including 60 percent of its softwood sawtimber (wood for building houses). Fourteen percent of American livestock, primarily cattle and sheep, graze in BLM districts or on other public land. The public lands, particularly in the Powder Ridge Basin in northeast Wyoming and southeast Montana, have a third of the nation's known coal reserve. A third of its uranium reserve is on public land in the Wyoming Basin and Colorado Plateau, 80 percent of its oil shale is on public land in the Green River Formation under Colorado, Utah, and Wyoming. Almost all large western ski resorts use Forest Service land. Public lands supply most of the nation's copper, silver, asbestos, lead, geothermal energy, brown and grizzly bears, caribou, bighorn sheep, moose, mule deer, and antelope; much of its oil, natural gas, antimony, beryllium, molybdenum, phosphate, and potash; and all its national parks, forests, wildlife refuges, and wilderness.

THE SURVIVAL OF THE FIEF

The federal lands are a gift of history: The federal government today owns nearly a third of the country because in the past it owned four-fifths. As one of the compromises leading to the signing of the Articles of Confederation—the 1781 predecessor to the Constitution—Connecticut, Georgia, Massachusetts, New York, North Carolina, South Carolina, and Virginia agreed to cede to the federal government their land claims beyond the Appalachians. These amounted to all or almost all of what is now Alabama, Illinois, Indiana, Michigan, Mississippi, Ohio, Tennessee, and Wisconsin. The federal government thus obtained its largest early stock of saleable public land. As the United States expanded across the continent, most of its land acquisitions entered the nation as public land that became part of territories and then states. The main western exceptions, Texas and Hawaii, previously had been independent nations with little public land on entry and little today: 2 and 10 percent of their area, respectively.

Behind slavery, the public lands were nineteenth-century America's dominant domestic issue. The 1803 Louisiana Purchase doubled the nation's size, added its present midsection, and more than tripled its stock of public land. Further acquisitions followed, for instance, the 1846 Oregon Compromise (Oregon, Idaho, Washington, and parts of Wyoming and Montana) from Britain; the 1848 Mexican Cession (California, Nevada, Utah, most of Arizona, parts of Colorado, New Mexico, and Wyoming); and the 1867 Alaska Purchase from Russia. The acquisitions had to be defended against not only the Indians, but also the British, French, Spanish, Mexicans, and Russians. The nation, its government and people desperately poor, needed what we now call economic development. Its eastern cities were full of immigrants with rural backgrounds, its eastern farms full of farmers who wanted better land. The territory from the Appalachians to the Pacific spelled personal and national opportunity. Nineteenth-century America called it Manifest Destiny.

So was born the largest regional development project in American history. The white settlement of the West was a huge real estate conveyance aimed at getting the public lands out of federal hands. The federal government happily cooperated in a long series of Sagebrush Rebellions, land sales, and land transfers. For more than the first century of the nation's existence, an actual majority of its federal laws dealt with the public holdings and their divestiture. Between 1818 and 1833, Alabama, Illinois, Indiana, Louisiana, and Missouri asked Congress to cede them all the federal land within their boundaries; and soon enough every midwestern and southern state, their residents, and their corporations got nearly all the land they wanted. The 1849 California and 1858 Colorado gold rushes occurred mainly on federal land, and were a totally illegal mass trespass. In the middle and late nineteenth century, the federal government gave Florida more than 24 million acres—nearly two-thirds of the state—and California, Oregon, and Washington got most of their public lands west of the Sierra-Cascades.

As the nineteenth century went on, claimants had to put up less money, could get more land and easier credit, had to do less with the land, were more likely to be able to avoid actually paying for it, and were less restrained—today we would say regulated—by the federal government. After the 1862 Homestead Act, individual claimants could get a plot of 160 acres for free if they signed an often nominal agreement to live on it for five years, farm it, and improve it. The federal government wanted the land settled, and was separated from it by nineteenth-century transportation and communication systems. It was a time of spectacular land fraud. The Manifest Destiny land rush was greedy, gory, grim: what the critic Vernon Parrington, one of the founders of American studies, called the Great Barbecue.

By the turn of the twentieth century, the land rush was subsiding. Its environmental excesses had been immense. The abundant herds of western buffalo, for instance, were extinguished within a few decades, as were billions of passenger pigeons and the upper Midwest pineries. In response the federal government began to set aside land for national parks in the 1870s, forests in the 1890s, wildlife refuges in the 1900s, and wildernesses in the 1920s. A great deal more western land proved nearly uninhabitable: most of the desert core between the Sierra-Cascades and the Rockies, also much of the Great Plains. The land allowed only scattered, physically and financially risky ranching and mining. The deepest desert in general had few takers, and they rarely lasted. It did not matter that the land was free; it was barren and waterless, with typically much less than 20 inches of rain a year. It could not be economically farmed, ranched, or otherwise occupied in 160-acre units or even—after the homesteading amount allowed for ranches was raised in the 1910s—640-acre ones.

Most western homesteading was wiped out by the small size of the farms and ranches, a train of droughts and rural depressions, and then the Great Depression. The bulk of the western homesteaders' abandoned holdings eventually passed into the hands of their neighbors or large, outside corporations or casually reverted to the federal government. In the end the federal government formally intervened: The 1934 Taylor Grazing Act abolished unsustainable, wishful-thinking homesteading by ending the large-scale disposals. It also established the present-day grazing districts and what soon became the BLM, and created the boundaries and legal form of most of today's public lands. The federal government today owns large parts of the West mainly by default, because the settlers rejected or could not cultivate the BLM lands, and to a lesser extent because it preserved the national forest, park, wildlife, and wilderness ones. Ninety-two percent of the western federal holdings have been public land for as long as they have been part of the United States. They are the leftovers of the Great Barbecue.

FORGETTING THE FIEF

After the end of homesteading and until the advent of James Watt, the public lands faded from the national consciousness. Both the lands and the federal possession of them became a side issue, an overlooked relic from frontier days. Marion Clawson, BLM director during the Truman administration and since at Resources for the Future, likes to tell of a surprise visit he had in 1950. Four highly competent Congressmen, all freshman Democrats from the New York City area, dropped by his BLM office with a simple, entirely friendly question: What were the public lands? "They had never heard," Clawson wrote in 1971, "of the Bureau of Land Management, or public domain, or grazing districts, or national forests, or national parks, or any of the laws under which the Bureau operates.... I'm afraid that, in a great deal of the United States, the Bureau is not much better known today than it was 20 years ago" (Clawson, 1971). The lands were not the compelling national concern they had been in the time of the pioneers. The fate of the public lands was no longer the fate of the West. The public lands were no longer the key to the American future.

James Watt and the Reagan administration did not change this situation appreciably, nor did they wish to. They sought to sell more holdings, unsuccessfully, for most of the western federal land is still almost unlivable, economically unattractive, and abundantly surrounded by more such land. The Sagebrush Rebellion was quickly revealed as a libertarian fantasy. The Reaganites were somewhat more effective in slowing acquisition (particularly of park and wildlife holdings), loosening regulation, and speeding development of public land. They were clearly, perhaps unintentionally, successful in reviving the sleepy field of public land policy: Many Americans who had not paid attention to the lands now did, for they distrusted what a right-wing development-oriented federal government might do with them. (When, in September 1982, the National Geographic Society issued an "America's Federal Lands" map, it rapidly and unexpectedly became one of the Society's all-time best sellers.)

The administration, for all its vast intentions of restoring traditional American values, has not been able to forge a coherent national consensus on how to deal with the public lands, by far the largest stretches of America that remain almost exactly as they were in 1800 or 1900. The administration has at most achieved an inchoate public sense that uncompromising preservation of all the lands may not always be the wisest approach. This vague stance is not in true conflict with the federal land agencies' ruling but equally vague policy of multiple use, which was first propounded by Gifford Pinchot when he was Theodore Roosevelt's forester. The administration has not been able nor has it tried to articulate a clear, convincing vision of what the public lands should be. Moreover, it has never offered an alternative to multiple use. (In January 1987, the Bureau of Land Management considered a trial-balloon proposal that would have explicitly declared the BLM an advocate of the minerals industry, but rejected the change.)

The old nineteenth-century rationales for American public land policy—expansion, defense, settlement, and economic development—no longer apply. They have not applied on a national scale for the bulk of this century or longer. No comparable, widely accepted rationales have replaced them. Multiple use does not remotely qualify. Indeed, it is something of a cop-out. It is a way of not having a national rationale for how to use the lands, of denying the need for one. It misdirects attention; it substitutes the undoubted, in fact, universal, worth of having a variety of uses possible on the land for the frequent necessity of choosing among them. It does not workably guide public decisions, nor is it clear how it could.

Thus at the heart of the nation's public land policy one finds a conceptual and operational void. It has existed for at least three generations. When in 1981–82 the administration sought to argue that selling some lands would help reduce the federal deficit—a perfectly respectable proposition in the 1830s—most public land professionals were politely amused. They evidently no longer considered the lands a likely place for policy innovations of national scope. The administration's proposals resurfaced in its first-draft fiscal 1987 budget, with even dimmer chances for adoption, for by then prices for the timber, cattle, sheep, mineral, and energy commodities the lands produce were at near-Depression levels, far below what they had been five years earlier. Once, it appeared, giants walked the public lands: explorers, Indians, missionaries, scouts, soldiers, trappers, traders, settlers, cowboys, boomers. Their present-day successors—federal civil servants, the employees of big timber, ranching, and mining operations, workers at large water projects, tourists, recreationists—do not seem to measure up. Once, when America was young, we knew why we had the lands. Now that America is mature, we mostly ignore them.

As a result, nearly all contemporary discussion of the lands seems stagnant, unable to move beyond ideas that were already cliches by World War II. On the political level, environmentalists and developers continue their disputes over the lands much as they did in 1910. Their positions have been hardened by generations of mutual suspicion, exaggerated claims, and a lack of fresh intellectual input. The interest groups on both sides often seem to regard their adversaries primarily as vehicles for their own fund-raising. Each side treats the lands largely as trophies to be kept from the other. The multiple-use policy encourages these attitudes and actions by allowing each side to think of the lands as places where anything is possible, including total victory over the other side. As Sierra Club lobbyist Timothy Mahoney told the American Land Resources Association's Agenda Project in 1984, "The mining lobby's attitude toward wilderness is, if they haven't found any minerals there yet then you can't put it aside as wilderness because they're still looking. If they do find minerals, then it can't be wilderness because it's their belief that there is no value as high as minerals" (American Land Forum, 1985).

Such misunderstandings and misrepresentations, deliberate and inadvertent, repeatedly recur all around. It is as if each side needs the other so that both may remain frozen in their mock-hostile, nationally unproductive postures. The multiple-use policy first helped create the century's environmentalist-developer struggle and then made it mainly fruitless, obstructionist. The consequence has been that, for several generations, America has failed to devise a new unified national idea of why it has the public lands and what it might do with them. But we need not accept the present impasse. There is a practical way to cut between the outmoded environmentalist and developer positions and go beyond them.

FINDING THE FIEF

In the late twentieth century, the public lands should be conceived as a nest egg, a federal reserve, a gigantic national land bank account put aside to meet America's future land needs. For now, the public lands simply constitute the great mythic West of big skies and cattle drives, lonesome roads and oasis towns, energy boomers and water shortages, cactus and steppe and tundra—"purple mountain majesties" that lack "the fruited plain." The public lands today are the heart of the remnant frontier, the seat of America's cowboy soul, a physically satisfying symbol of the nation's romance with the range. Yet there may come a time when the country will want to draw on its nest egg or land reserve, when it will, for example, need a now-undiscovered mineral found only on the public lands, or have to use the lands for some agricultural, defense, energy, or environmental purpose unknowable today. The more prevalent privately owned lands might also serve such purposes, but the public lands could be more likely because of the comparative difficulty of publicly influencing the uses of private property or taking it under eminent domain.

Put more gravely, the country may someday face a national emergency to which the public lands will be the primary solution. During the 1973–81 energy crisis, Alaska–then 96 percent in federal hands— served this function to some degree; but the performance could become more obvious if the peril were worse. Generations from now, the nation may rediscover the public lands and desperately want to settle or otherwise use them: the year after a major West Coast earthquake, a nuclear disaster, overwhelming population pressure from Latin America, a hazardous waste crisis, or an unknowable economic, military, biological, or climatic event. If the emergency never comes, well enough since there was no alternative use for much of the land anyway.

The extent to which the public lands are essentially ownerless, passively operated, and thus available as a federal nest egg or reserve is rarely appreciated. According to the Bureau of Land Management's *Public Land Statistics 1983*, the BLM as the main federal custodian held 341 million western acres, about 15 percent of the United States. Less than half this land, 157 million acres, was in BLM's grazing districts, the most prevalent use of its holdings and a low intensity one. (Most of the rest was in bush Alaska, in even less intense use.) Moreover, not all the grazing allotments were used—or were worth using—by the ranchers and sheep raisers who rented them at cheap rates (more precisely, federally subsidized ones).

Vast areas of the public lands—most particularly, the BLM holdings—are beautiful but poor: infertile, scrub-arid, isolated, rocky, far from utility lines, desert, mountainous, or arctic. They are America's outback, form much of the West's proverbial wide-open spaces, and have been largely neglected since the closing of the frontier. The lands were only lightly used by the Indians. Few whites ever learned how to use them, and today we can find no use for them other than often marginal grazing. But if a national land emergency does come, the lands will massively reenter American history.

Consider one possible nest-egg scenario. The federal government may eventually respond to the permanent decline of Northeast, Midwest, and West Coast heavy industry, and to some future mounting demand for American agricultural products abroad, by aggressively encouraging western homesteading by reopening it in selected areas. Many displaced workers have mechanical skills, agricultural backgrounds, and a desire to leave the big cities, just as the first homesteaders did. The new homesteading might also attract the Hispanic, Oriental, and southern European immigrants now flooding some cities, especially western ones. Many of the nation's family farmers and ranchers, now being foreclosed in increasing numbers, might welcome a second chance on a government claim.

Serious federal encouragement of reopened homesteading would probably require individual tracts for larger than 160 or 640 acres. (John Wesley Powell [1878] in his prophetic report had recommended a minimum of 2,560 acres, 4 square miles.) Revived homesteading would also demand good coordination with state public land agencies. It would definitely require federal support and training for the water, credit, transportation, equipment, and marketing mechanisms the new homesteads would need. It would be an expensive undertaking, but a better national investment than unproductively letting the potential homesteaders rot in the cities and elsewhere (and draw federal funds such as welfare) as the deterioration of the nation's industrial base worsens. Possibly fruitful areas for the new homesteading might be the eastern slopes of the Cascades in the Northwest, the eastern slopes of the Sierras in central California, the western Rio Grande Valley in New Mexico, or central Alaska—where the Interior Department in fact experimentally reopened homesteading in the Kuskokwim Mountains in 1982.

THE FUNCTION OF THE FIEF

As a national nest egg, the public lands should represent a store set aside in anticipation of unspecified times of trouble or need. The point of the public lands, as with a nest egg, should not be to spend the contents as quickly as possible, which is, however, just about what most developers favoring large-scale exploitation, disposal, or deregulation would have us do. This prototypical developer position—currently that of large parts of the federal government also—is wastefully foolish, too quick to liquidate the holdings. But neither is the point necessarily to save all the holdings as long as possible, which is what most environmentalists favoring large-scale preservation, expansion, or regulation would want. The prototypical environmentalist position is retentively foolish, too hesitant to liquidate; concrete current needs (for energy, say) may sometimes be legitimately more pressing than abstract future ones.

Instead the point, again as with a nest egg, should be to maintain the federal land reserve so that it provides a satisfactory margin against future demands. Such a position falls between the environmentalist and developer extremes. In keeping up its reserve, the nation would almost certainly exploit, dispose of, or deregulate some holdings while it preserves, expands, or regulates others. It could spend the public lands at the same time that it saves them. It could save some holdings and spend them later, or vice versa. It could enlarge or contract the reserve to react to external events: environmentalist upswings, economic downturns, minerals shortages, other predictable surprises of national development.

To employ the nest-egg approach, we need only make sure that the reserve's continuing margin remains prudently generous: not a difficult requirement, given the vastness and diversity of America's public land dowry. This approach would represent the true spirit of conservation and wise use, as distinct from the environmentalist and developer ones. The approach would also allow the satisfaction of many environmentalist and developer land demands, although not all of them, just as a nest egg permits the satisfaction of many, but not all, saving and spending impulses. The approach would frequently allow the continuation of the present multiple-use policy.

The concept of the public lands as a national nest egg is not novel. Neither is the idea that the overall nest egg can be replenished and diminished simultaneously in response to new land needs or unexpected land emergencies. Indeed, when the brute imperatives of circumstance have obliged us to abandon doctrinaire all-or-nothing preservation or exploitation approaches to the public lands—that is, when hitherto unimagined uses for them emerged—the nation and its land agencies frequently, perhaps typically, adopted nest-egg measures.

For instance, much of the legislation that established the lands was intended to replenish the reserve so as to forestall future land difficulties. The first national forests were created in 1891 in part to anticipate a timber shortage that supposedly loomed for the turn of the century. Later national forests, along with the national parks, wildlife refuges, and wildernesses, were (and still are being) set aside in order that the nation would not run short of such beautiful lands; as a result, it now has the world's most impressive system of them. The Taylor Grazing Act instituted grazing districts and many of the rest of today's public land devices to prevent persistently disastrous homesteading. Similar federal replenishment impulses motivated the creation in the 1920s of northwest Alaska's National Petroleum Reserve, southern California's and central Wyoming's Naval Petroleum Reserves, and eastern Utah's Naval Oil Shale Reserve.

Other, equally sensible policies diminished the federal land reserve so as to meet emerging land demands. The Homestead Act is the most obvious instance. Moreover, on several occasions since the Taylor Act, the federal government relaxed its prohibition on homesteading to promote settlement near federal projects such as dams; for example, in the late 1940s homesteaders occupied nearly 200,000 acres of irrigated farms in southwest Arizona's Gila River project near Yuma. Under the 1971 Alaska Native Claims Settlement Act, the nation gave 44 million acres and almost a billion dollars to the state's Native Americans to make up for what it had done to the Lower 48 ones (as well as to extinguish any other indigenous Alaskan claims). The Reagan administration has sold federal land ringing western cities such as Albuquerque, Anchorage, and Las Vegas to keep the holdings from constricting their rapid growth. It has shown a willingness to make similar sales around the western energy boomtowns of the 1970s if their now-busted economies revive. Its fiscal 1987 budget proposals envisioned selling the California and Wyoming Naval Petroleum Reserves.

The country has historically leased federal land to mineral developers, including oil and natural gas companies, on terms so loose as to amount to selling (or even giving) it to them.

In light of this long, often explicit use of nest-egg approaches, it should not be difficult to formally incorporate them into public land policies. The federal land agencies need not alter much of their existing operations and goals. They need not do anything precipitous or immediate, let alone anything regulatory. Much of the multiple-use policy could remain in place. But the agencies should do more to explore the federal land reserve, to find out what the nation's public land assets actually are.

For instance, the federal government's primary maps of the public lands, those produced by the Interior Department's Geological Survey, are widely acknowledged by their users to be perhaps three-quarters accurate; they ought to be improved. Large chunks of the public lands have yet to be fully explored: for example, the northern Snake River Valley in Idaho, the Wah Wah Mountains in western Utah, Monument Valley in northern Arizona, the Wrangell Mountains in southern Alaska, the Brooks Range in northern Alaska, and the Owyhee River Canyons near the intersection of Oregon, Idaho, and Nevada. The Alaska mountains—to take the case of the nation's largest stretches of effectively uncharted land—contain hundreds of peaks over 10,000 feet that have never been named, much less climbed. The BLM, the main trustee of such places, should be more active in exploring them—not opening them up to oil companies or tourists, but simply learning what is there.

Alaska, for instance, the sixth of America that bulks so large in western development plans, will still be three-fifths federal land after the disposals mandated by the Native Claims Act, the 1958 Statehood Act, and the 1980 Alaska National Interest Lands Conservation Act are complete, probably by 1990. The state's public land has—and after 1990 will mostly retain—a quarter of the nation's coal reserves, half its supply of fresh water, huge stores of natural gas, a surprisingly bountiful agricultural potential, and hundreds of uncharted, untrod mountains and valleys. If necessary, the state could produce as much oil in the next ten years as the Lower 48 states have since the first well in Titusville, Pennsylvania, in 1859.

In the 1980s we have an American North almost as large, uninhabited, virginal, rich, and environmentally vulnerable as the American West was in the 1870s. We also have extraordinarily little hard information about even its most lucrative natural resources, its minerals. As Malcolm Baldwin of the American Bar Association told the American Land Resource Association's Agenda Project in 1984, there are "good [minerals] people who say that we simply don't know what is available up in Alaska" (Mahoney, 1985). We obviously have an immense amount, but no idea exactly how much. The American Petroleum Institute's John Peschke told the Project, "You don't know what's there until you punch a hole in the ground" (Mahoney, 1985). Not enough of those holes are being punched, by minerals industries or others, in Alaska or the Lower 48. The federal land agencies should be encouraging more hole punching, keeping closer track of the results, and making more certain that the environmental consequences are not objectionable.

Some form of national land budgeting might well be feasible, at least for the public lands (American Land Forum, 1982). Even rudimentary land budgeting for the public holdings would facilitate their use as a sort of economic safety valve to draw off excesses of demand on private land. Suppose, as may happen someday, western land demands for housing, urban growth, coals, or other minerals come to compete so intensely with alternative demands for private land that they create painful increases in land prices, environmental damage, or commodity shortfalls in the West. Then the housing, urban, coal, or mineral demand might be purposefully channeled to carefully selected public lands, probably BLM holdings. This approach might help preserve ranching and other western agriculture, which are traditionally risky and now under special pressure from falling agricultural prices and (in some places) competing land uses. It would allow the housing, urban, coal, or mineral demands to be satisfied. It would amount to a foresighted reduction in the federal nest egg.

THE FUTURE FIEF

The nest egg will certainly be depleted in coming years by the Alaska disposals and smaller scale ones, but I suspect that during the same period the overall level of the reserve will rise. The federal government may acquire a great deal more western land, this time east of the Rockies, in the Great Plains. It now has relatively small holdings in the Plains, that is, eastern Montana, Wyoming, Colorado, and New Mexico, and western North Dakota, South Dakota, Nebraska, Kansas, Oklahoma, and Texas. But farming—whether for cotton, cattle, or corn, sheep, wheat, or hogs—is dying throughout much of the Plains because of lack of water, distance from markets, and particularly the downturn in farm prices. Just as in the 1890s and 1930s, nature and the economy have cyclically turned hostile. The Plains promise to become again one of the great failure sectors of American agriculture.

The difficulties of Plains farming have historically been far worse than those of its neighbor region to the east, the Midwest's Corn Belt. Even now, despite the genuine, well-publicized problems Corn Belt farmers face, they at least have water and are comparatively close to markets. No replacement crops, federal subsidies, or foreseeable irrigation techniques are likely to save Plains farming. The Plains could undergo a large-scale 1930s-style Depression, complete with Dust Bowls. Much of the Plains is already losing population rapidly, especially young people, becoming a place of old people and disappearing farms. There will certainly be an uncomfortable number of farm bankruptcies and an unacceptable amount of farmland erosion. Both will be distinctly more severe than in the Midwest.

The federal government reacted to the 1930s Plains agricultural crisis, which in fact produced less soil erosion than is occurring today, by buying out 5 million acres of farm holdings, an area the size of New Hampshire. The government turned these acres into the national grasslands that are now administered by the Forest Service: locally unusable, nationally unneeded cropland that was turned back into the open prairie the settlers found in the nineteenth century. During the 1930s, the Forest Service sought to return 17 million more Plains acres to national grasslands. Franklin Roosevelt's Interior Secretary Harold Ickes urged that the federal government acquire still other substantial areas such as the entire Oklahoma Panhandle, at almost 6,600 square miles bigger than three Delawares.

As the Ogallala Aquifer runs dry, as other Plains agriculture succumbs in a strip 200 to 700 miles wide across the country's midsection, and as outmigration from the Plains increases, the nation may conclude that this part of America should never have been farmed, settled, or even privatized in the first place. (It might not have been were it on the western edge of the continent rather than in its center.) If Plains agriculture did not exist, the winning argument will go, it would not have to be invented. Nor would its operation, particularly its irrigation, have to be heavily and inefficiently supported by the federal government. Federal agencies will then offer incentives deliberately aimed at dismantling large pieces of Plains agriculture, at speeding the depopulation of the Plains. The federal nest egg will be drastically enlarged.

THE FATE OF THE FIEF

In 1852, Massachusetts's Daniel Webster professed to be repelled by the American Southwest. "What," he thundered, "do we want with this worthless area, this region of savages and wild beasts, of shifting sands and whirlwinds of dust, of cactus and prairie dogs? To what use could we ever hope to put these great deserts and these endless mountain ranges?" The aged orator could see no point to the lands wrested from Mexico in 1848: what are today California, Nevada, Utah, most of Arizona, and parts of Colorado, New Mexico, and Wyoming. As a skeptic of western expansion, Webster—defender of the rising industries of the Northeast, opponent of the Mexican War, enemy of the spread of slavery into the West—did not even acknowledge what the 1849 California gold rush had already contributed to the nation's development.

Webster showed uncharacteristically little insight into the future. He could not, of course, have anticipated federal irrigation, massive energy and timber development, the cities of the Sunbelt West, the national parks, the BLM, eastern tourism, the environmental movement, the cattle, agribusiness, and aerospace industries, the rise of California, or any of the other forces that have shaped the Pacific side of America. He nonetheless seems singularly shortsighted and self-centered. Because he could not imagine uses for the West, he imagined that there never would be any. Because the West had not yet really been used by Americans, it never would be. Because it did not appeal to him, it would not appeal to his contemporaries or to future generations of Americans. Many prominent Americans had comparable doubts about Jefferson's 1803 purchase of Louisiana for four cents an acre. Many Americans felt similarly dubious about Secretary of State William Seward's 1867 purchase of Alaska ("Seward's Folly") for two cents an acre.

We should not make the same mistake about the West's public lands. We may not be able to conceive of uses for immense tracts of the holdings, but our successors almost certainly will. Our duty to them is to maintain the federal nest egg as generously as we can, so as not to foreclose their options. We can best render stewardship to the lands by preserving them as a factor for the American future. The public lands have an enduring resonance in the American psyche. They will always have meaning for what they are and were. But they have a different significance—one must assume a greater one—for what they might be decades or centuries from now. We should do little, preferably nothing, that would diminish this other import. This approach should supplant the prototypical developer and environmentalist ones, as well as the multiple-use policy that permits them to flourish. The nest-egg approach should become public land policy's commanding idea.

It would be ironic if the age-encrusted, intricate struggles between environmentalists and developers for control of the public lands through the mechanism of multiple use were to give way to a simpler, less pressured concern about maintaining the federal nest egg. It would also be a healthy evolution. The reptilian-intense disputes of environmentalists and developers, especially their battles to have the last say on multiple use, have not served the country well for many years. In particular, they have divided much of it uselessly and prevented the emergence of alternative perspectives on the public lands. If the disputes dissolved into—or even were informed by—a more human, more relaxed, less nationally acrimonious effort to conserve the public land nest egg, the country as a whole would be better off.

The environmentalist and developer approaches each have made a worthwhile contribution to public land policies, but neither can now pretend to be anything other than a partial guide for them. Moreover, by themselves the approaches are not truly complementary: standing alone, they cannot legitimately be brought into any clear or stable balance, despite the multiple-use policy and most of our century's other public land devices. Individually, they are always limited, usually outdated, and typically hard to reconcile with each other. They need an overarching framework, a conceptual armature, to move between them and align them into coherent national policy. The idea of the federal nest egg or land reserve provides such a framework.

It also offers a way to rehabilitate multiple use. The policy, as presently used, is not really a policy. It is a term of art that begins by meaning all things to all parties and ends up meaning nothing to anyone. Yet a great deal of public land law in fact defines multiple use in terms that amount to the nest-egg approach. The prime public land statute, for instance, the 1976 Federal Land Policy and Management Act, states that multiple use must avoid "permanent impairment of the productivity of the land and the quality of the environment," should "allow for periodic adjustments in use to conform to changing needs and conditions," and "take into account the long-term needs of future generations."

Unfortunately, almost no one notices this binding language, much less takes it seriously. We should. One of the few observers who does, Paul Culhane of the University of Houston, argues that "practical multiple use" means that "an optimum use in any given area is the highest level of use that does not foreclose the possibility of other uses by diminishing the capability of the land to provide them in perpetuity" (Culhane, 1981). This is precisely the nest-egg approach. Perhaps one could call it meta-multiple use. This revised, revived version of multiple use demands long-run sustainability. It requires the purposeful integration of environmental and developmental needs, very much in the manner of René Dubos.

Jefferson went ahead with the controversial Louisiana Purchase largely because he believed that Americans would need 100 generations to settle the West and discover its uses, but then would be sustained by it for 1,000 generations. Seven generations later, he may have been more prescient than we realize. The United States has immensely more land, especially public land, than it can now use. The theme of excess space runs through the history of every western state. The public lands are part of our endowment, one of the reasons we remain a lucky country. Webster asked the permanent questions of American land history: What would the uses of the West prove to be? What can we do with our enormous, apparently useless public holdings? His answer was crabbed, unimaginative: We could do nothing with the West and its public lands, ever. Jefferson had a more flexible, expansive answer: We might not know what to do with them, but our descendants would. So the best heritage we can give them is that we leave the choices open to them. Maintaining the federal nest egg and reanimating multiple use require no great managerial or predictive ability, only the wisdom to know that the future will be different.

Bibliography

American Land Forum. 1985. "The Great Public Lands Debate" (Winter): 17.
————. 1982. "Toward a National Land Budget" (Spring).
Bureau of Land Management, U.S. Department of the Interior. 1984. *Public Land Statistics 1983*. Washington, D.C.: U.S. Government Printing Office.
Clawson, Marion. 1971. *The Bureau of Land Management*. New York: Praeger, pp. viii–ix.
Culhane, Paul. 1981. *Public Lands Politics: Interest Group Influence on the Forest Service and the Bureau of Land Management*. Baltimore: Johns Hopkins University Press for Resources for the Future, p. 307.
Popper, Frank J. 1984. "The Timely End of the Sagebrush Rebellion." *The Public Interest* (Summer).
Powell, John Wesley. 1878. "Report on the Lands of the Arid Region of the United States, with a More Detailed Account of the Lands of Utah." House Executive Document No. 73, 45th Congress, 2nd Session, Washington, D.C.

8

THE CONSEQUENCES OF CHANGE WITHOUT DIALOGUE: AN HISTORIC PRESERVATION PERSPECTIVE

Don L. Klima

ABSTRACT

Any discourse on the social implications of land-use management must come to terms with the role of the citizenry in decision making. Although national policy, as articulated in federal environmental statutes, has firmly established the importance of adequate public involvement in planning, public participation has too often been reduced to form at the expense of substance. While this dilemma poses serious consequences for all land-use decisions, this chapter examines the particular problems associated with public participation in those situations where urban development proposals conflict with community goals to conserve neighborhoods and protect historic resources. By use of a case study—the Presidential Parkway in Atlanta, Georgia—it examines the barriers to effective citizen involvement and suggests possible remedies.

Key Words: historic preservation, neighborhood conservation, Advisory Council on Historic Preservation, public participation, Section 106 of the National Historic Preservation Act

A SENSE OF PLACE

Modern industrial technology, by offering the technical means for mass production, has democratized material culture. Experiences, products, and amenities that were previously the province of a limited few have now become commonplace. While quantitative multiplication of artifacts has enormously extended individual opportunity, its profoundly disturbing effects on both the environment and cultural adaptation are all too well known. Writing in his classic text, *Historic Preservation: Curatorial Management of the Built Environment*, James Fitch sees historic preservation as one logical and necessary response to the dehumanizing aspects of the industrial age (Fitch, 1982). In addition to the educational and patriotic values often associated with historic preservation, its effort to salvage the prototypical and original as a counterpoint to the spreading homogeneity of the visual landscape most accounts for its growing popularity. It is "a sense of place," a phrase that now ranks as the movement's anthem, that best expresses the intrinsic value of historic resources as stabilizing features in our environment.

The desire to somehow capture a feeling of permanence by preserving tangible remains from the past has known no geographic boundaries, from the Lahaina Historic District on the west of Maui to the Lowell Historic Mill Complex in Massachusetts; no temporal boundaries, from the Dulles International Airport to the remains of early man at the Clovis Site in New Mexico; no technological boundaries, from Launch Complex 39 at Kennedy Space Center to the San Francisco Cable Car network; no demographic boundaries, from the Colonial Germantown Historic District in Philadelphia to the rural Nacoochee Valley in northern Georgia. It is the persistent efforts of historic preservation advocates, sometimes allied with efforts to protect the natural environment, that have helped effect a fundamental change in how Americans perceive and feel about their surroundings. Once relegated to Fourth of July celebrations, our history has emerged as a benevolent force in shaping the image of our cities, communities, and farmlands.

FEDERAL RESPONSE TO THE HISTORIC PRESERVATION ACT

The major federal legislative framework for the historic preservation movement was established with passage of the National Historic Preservation Act in 1966. In the act, Congress declared, among other things, that:

the historical and cultural foundations of the Nation should be preserved as a living part of our community life and developed in order to give a sense of orientation to the American people; [and that] . . . the preservation of this irreplaceable heritage is in the public interest so that its vital legacy of cultural, educational, aesthetic, inspirational, economic, and energy benefits will be maintained and enriched for future generations of Americans.

The act was an important forerunner to the watershed environmental legislation that would soon follow: the National Environmental Policy

Act, the Clean Water Act, and the Clean Air Act, all of which sought to change the role of the federal government from passive observer to active participant, partner, and catalytic agent. In the case of the National Historic Preservation Act, a state-federal alliance was formed. The federal government would provide technical assistance and money, while states were to carry out the task of identifying historic and archeological properties in each state and begin planning for their recognition and protection.

The act also sought to address an underlying series of potential conflicts. While the importance of historic resources to the nation's psyche had been both tacitly and vocally acknowledged, the federal government had been carrying out an array of activities that systematically removed these features from the landscape. Well-intended yet single-minded plans to remake cities in the suburban image led to a direct assault by urban renewal on the nation's historic urban cores. Archeological deposits offering invaluable evidence of prehistoric peoples were destroyed by the thousands to make way for flood control reservoirs and interstate highway projects. In no realm did these threats seem more pervasive than on federal lands, where federal agencies acted at best indifferent and at worst antagonistic toward national preservation goals.

In the National Historic Preservation Act, Congress attempted to set federal policy on a new course by charging federal agencies to act in concert with, rather than at cross-purposes with, historic preservation goals and to take the lead in developing a spirit of stewardship for the country's historic resources. To encourage and help oversee this hoped for transformation, the act established the Advisory Council on Historic Preservation, and in Section 106 directed federal agencies to work with the council to take the effects of their diverse activities on historic resources into account in their planning and decision making.

Through its oversight and consultative role, the council has been involved during the past 20 years in the review of literally thousands of federal and federally assisted projects. Consider the ambitious efforts of the federal government to transform our society and its infrastructure during this time. The last two decades have witnessed the construction of wastewater treatment plants and facilities, virtual completion of the interstate highway system, construction of major water and flood control projects, redevelopment of our cities through a broad range of assistance programs (for example, rapid rail systems, housing, and infrastructure), support of energy production, minerals management and extraction, development of new defense installations, agricultural production and soil conservation initiatives, and park and recreation facility enhancement.

At the same time, federal responsibilities for ongoing management and use of millions of acres of federal lands have continued unabated. All of these activities, as well as the ancillary permitting and licensing actions of agencies as diverse in purpose and method as the U.S. Army Corps of Engineers, the Federal Home Loan Bank Board, and the Federal Energy Regulatory Commission have, in some form or another, given birth to conflicts between development and historic resources. Because these conflicts have consequently required council review and involvement under Section 106, the council has been in a unique position to observe how effectively federal agencies have or have not involved the public in planning and decision making.

THE PUBLIC'S ROLE

The legislative and judicial processes giving us the evolving corpus of environmental statutes during the past 20 years have reinforced the belief that citizens have a right to participate in federal decision making which affects the environment. Opinions by the courts have consistently upheld this fundamental right. The National Environmental Policy Act—the nation's basic charter for protection of the environment, along with its implementing regulations—establishes the policy that agencies must encourage and facilitate public involvement in decisions which affect the quality of the environment. However, it fails to state the mechanism by which this is to be accomplished. Thus it has been left to the agencies themselves, through a broad range of procedures, to provide the means and methods for involving the public.

Likewise, the National Historic Preservation Act directs agencies to approach their historic preservation responsibilities in partnership with states, local governments, Indian tribes, private organizations, and individuals. Thus the council's regulations, "Protection of Historic and Cultural Properties," which are directed at implementing Section 106, have always encouraged maximum public participation. As a matter of policy, it has been believed that federal agencies have an affirmative responsibility to engage the public in deciding which properties are significant, how they may be affected by proposed actions, and what measures should be taken in response to potential impacts. The regulations further make it clear that the council must weigh the views of the public in its overall review, as well as in developing specific solutions that will avoid or mitigate the effects of an action on historic resources.

ATLANTA'S PLANNED PRESIDENTIAL PARKWAY

Perhaps no other single case in the council's recent experience better illustrates the barriers, both methodological and substantive, to effective public involvement than the proposed construction of the Presidential Parkway in Atlanta, Georgia. The parkway controversy has sharply divided the city, pitted former political allies against one another, become a *cause celèbre* for civil disobedience, and led the courts to declare Georgia's longstanding development practices unconstitutional. The parkway case vividly illustrates the mutual support that often arises between the historic preservation and neighborhood conservation movements, as well as the galvanizing effect that they can collectively have on civic activism. For those concerned with land-use planning, the parkway controversy offers a warning about the political paralysis that can result when public policy making is divorced from the public.

The Emergence of Conflicting Goals: The Presidential Parkway—Library or Neighborhood Conservation

In a real sense, public opposition to the Presidential Parkway proposal has been 20 years in the making. In the 1960s, the Georgia Department of Transportation (DOT) proposed constructing two major highways east of Atlanta's central business district: I–485, which would connect with existing interstates, and the Stone Mountain Tollway, which would provide access between the downtown and the growing suburbs in the northeast. Neighborhoods threatened by these projects joined forces. Through a combination of successful court action under the National Environmental Policy Act and political pressure that led Governor Jimmy Carter to withdraw his support for the projects, both proposals were killed during the 1970s.

Unfortunately, this happened too late to stop Georgia DOT's acquisition and "clearance" of over 700 residences and businesses from the now unneeded rights-of-way. Some of the vacant land was later transferred and redeveloped, but Georgia DOT retained ownership to a 219-acre corridor. For over 10 years, the future of this corridor has been in limbo, with Georgia DOT continuing to argue that a transportation facility is needed, while citizens have been equally adamant that the land should revert to passive use and be developed as a park.

Only recently did the impetus shift to Georgia DOT's position, when former President Carter entered the debate with plans to construct his presidential library in Atlanta. Civic leaders led by Mayor Andrew Young, a long-time Carter supporter, were understandably eager to have Carter's library in Atlanta. While most citizens and civic leaders agreed that the vacant highway corridor close to the downtown was an ideal location for the library, Georgia DOT countered by citing a host of state and federal statutes prescribing the legal disposition of previously acquired right-of-way. The agency would make every effort to cooperate, but only if a highway project were the centerpiece of the redevelopment plan.

While the fate of the corridor remained undecided for over a decade, many of the neighborhoods surrounding the corridor underwent a dramatic physical, political, and social transformation. These neighborhoods, offering both proximity to the city center and housing stock that is architecturally distinctive, had gradually attracted families who were disenchanted with the isolation of newer suburbs. With growing investment and increasing revitalization success, new homeowners joined with long-time residents to become an active political force. In various ways, they sought to convince city hall that their neighborhoods contributed to the vitality, diversity, and livability of the city and should be protected.

To give focus to their arguments and anchor community pride, homeowners frequently sought recognition of their neighborhoods' historic qualities and thus allied themselves with the growing historic preservation movement taking place throughout the city. The seven neighborhoods bordering the highway corridor—from the small frame Victorian houses in the Old Fourth Ward nearest the downtown to the more substantial architectural eclecticism of Druid Hills at the city limits—illustrate the progressive development of Atlanta's suburbs from the late nineteenth century to the Depression. Residents of these neighborhoods, remembering earlier successes in defeating unwanted highways and united by a common goal, once again began to organize to form a united front in opposition to the Presidential Parkway proposal.

Meanwhile, Georgia DOT, with promised funding assistance from the Federal Highway Administration (FHWA), moved forward with its proposal. The composite plan that emerged called for a four-lane urban arterial to be constructed, with associated recreational amenities (bike and jogging trails, playgrounds, and picnic areas) dispersed along the right-of-way. The parkway would connect with an interstate highway stub near the eastern edge of the central business district, extend northeastward, and terminate at Ponce de Leon Avenue in the Druid Hills area about 2.4 miles away and, according to highway planners, the new road would relieve commuter traffic in adjacent residential areas. While called a "parkway," the road's design featured 20-foot cuts, several major bridge structures, and pavement widths of up to 80 feet. Through a cooperative agreement in which the city would arrange to make land available for lease or purchase through a land exchange with Georgia DOT, a 30-acre tract would be set aside for construction of the Carter Presidential Library and Museum and the Carter Center of Emory University. Additional surrounding green space would be considered a "roadside amenity." For its part, the city proposed to acquire through lease or exchange with Georgia DOT the remaining remnant land parcels in the corridor for construction of up to 700 housing units to help replace those previously demolished.

The Public Reacts

Promising a Presidential Library, replacement housing, and recreation facilities, the city and Georgia DOT took their plans to the public hoping that opposition to the highway would be undercut. Judged solely by surface appearances and by the volume of comment, the attempts by the city and Georgia DOT to solicit the public's views were impressive. Beginning in early 1982, Mayor Young formed a multidisciplinary team to conduct public scoping meetings with citizens, groups, and state and federal officials. Project opponents charged that the scoping process, billed by Mayor Young as an aggressive attempt to involve the public in planning, was instead a carefully calculated public relations campaign to sell the project to potential supporters while giving only passing notice to both general neighborhood concerns and project opponents. Georgia DOT endorsed the city's efforts and formally adopted the results of the city's scoping process in lieu of independently conducted efforts.

Following release of the draft environmental impact statement in April 1983, Georgia DOT and FHWA conducted a series of three public information meetings in neighborhoods adjacent to the project. These meetings did little to dispel neighborhood fears that the project was a foregone conclusion. On arriving, citizens found detailed project plans displayed, Georgia DOT personnel to answer questions, and a court reporter to "officially" record their comments—hardly an atmosphere conducive to a constructive dialogue on the merits of the project. By June 1983, public opposition to the project had reached the boiling point; a crowd estimated at over 3,000 persons attended the final public information meeting that was held at the Atlanta Civic Center. Many picketed outside.

When the commenting period closed, Georgia DOT had received written comments from 728 individuals and organizations, some of which included signed petitions with more than 700 signatures. The public record filled over 17 large volumes. Eleven of these were comprised of letters, and the remaining six contained transcripts of testimony from the various public hearing and meetings.

Had public comment on the parkway been treated as a referendum, plans for its construction would probably have been promptly placed on a shelf to gather dust. Ninety percent of the comments expressed opposition to the project. While many commenters expressed concern about specific problems such as the street closings and school bus route changes the road would necessitate and the volume of traffic it would generate, the essential public sentiment was that the highway would be an alienating feature on the landscape, incompatible with the qualities and characteristics of the surrounding neighborhoods as residential areas.

Equally telling was the virtual lack of public commentary in support of the project's principal justification: relieving congestion on local neighborhood streets by providing a direct link to the downtown from the suburbs. Just as citizens spoke as one in their opposition to the road, they were equally united in their support for Carter's library. However, most doubted that the road was needed to provide access to the library, and many of those voicing support for the road appear to have done so out of fear that the library plans would be jeopardized if the road was stopped.

The Council Response

The council first entered this maelstrom in March 1983 when it received letters from several neighborhood organizations expressing concern that FHWA had not met its responsibilities under Section 106 of the National Historic Preservation Act. Following an exchange of letters, FHWA initiatied the Section 106 process some eight months later in November 1983 by providing the council with extensive information on the project and requesting council comments. Based on this initial review, it was concluded that the parkway would have a wide range of impacts, both direct and indirect, on the various historic districts. However, the most serious consequences would be experienced in the Candler Park Historic District and the Druid Hills Historic District, where new right-of-way for construction was required.

The implications for the Druid Hills Historic District were of particular concern. Conceived and planned on a grand scale and designed by Frederick Law Olmsted, who was the founder of landscape architecture in America, Druid Hills represents the apex of early twentieth-century residential development, not only in Atlanta but throughout the South. The parkway would intrude literally into the heart of Olmsted's plan and contravene some of the most important aspects of his design, the careful placement of picturesque and formal parks and the undulating, integrated road network. In addition, development of the parkway would inescapably lead to the widening of Ponce de Leon Avenue eastward, which had long been advocated by Georgia DOT. The consequences of such widening would be even more damaging to Olmsted's design of the curving avenue, its bordering green spaces, and its associated neighborhood qualities.

To mitigate these impacts, the council proposed a compromise: The parkway be terminated at Moreland Avenue just west of Candler Park, and that comprehensive consideration be given to associated traffic improvements that would meet the expressed transportation needs (for example, intersection improvements; wider turn lanes on Moreland Avenue; and the use of reversible rush hour lanes, signing, and signalization improvements for Ponce de Leon Avenue and other local commuter routes). Georgia DOT rejected this proposal as insufficient. With little hope that further discussions would lead to a resolution acceptable to all parties, Alexander Aldrich, then chairman of the council, decided that the full council should review the case.

On February 27, 1983, the council met in Atlanta in public session. Following a presentation of the project by FHWA and Georgia DOT and supporting testimony from Mayor Young, the council members toured the project corridor and historic districts. The visit included an on-site meeting with former President Carter to learn firsthand of his plans for the library and policy center. When the meeting reconvened that afternoon in public session, the council received public testimony. Over 900 citizens attended the meeting, and public testimony lasted well into the night. As in the earlier public record, elected state representatives, members of the city council, neighborhood and civic organizations, and individuals articulated—often in very personal terms—their strong conviction that the highway should not be built.

Following public testimony, the council members deliberated on the evidence they had received and voted 12 to 4 to recommend that FHWA not support construction of the project. In further recommendations, the council urged that Georgia DOT—in cooperation with former President Carter, the city, and affected neighborhood organizations—explore all feasible options for establishment of the Carter Library Complex while making use of local streets and the MARTA (Metropolitan Atlanta Rapid Transit Authority) public transit system for effective visitor access. The council strongly supported those aspects of the plan calling for development of recreational facilities and reestablishment of housing compatible with surrounding neighborhoods.

The satisfaction felt by the opponents over the outcome of the council's review was regrettably short-lived. After providing its recommendations to the U.S. Department of Transportation, the council was notified that the department had decided to fund the project regardless of the council's advice. Under Section 106 of the National Historic Preservation Act, a federal agency is only required to take into account the comments of the council; having done so, it can then make its own decision on the course of action it will take.

Failing administrative remedies, the succeeding months saw the project opponents turn to the courts to stop the road. At the state level, a complicated series of rulings in the county courts leading to a Georgia Supreme Court appeal resulted in the judicial finding that Georgia DOT had no power to condemn public property and, therefore, could not acquire 8.6 acres of city-owned park land for the road project. This ruling not only cast Georgia DOT's plans for the parkway into doubt, it also found state agency condemnation of publicly owned lands unconstitutional—a situation that will require action by the state legislature. Meanwhile, the U.S. Court of Appeals for the Eleventh Circuit ruled that FHWA had inadequately demonstrated that there were no prudent and feasible alternatives to the taking of parklands and had thus failed to meet the requirements of Section 4(f) of the Department of Transportation Act. In response to this ruling, FHWA had to prepare an addendum to its environmental assessment. As a consequence of this litigation, construction on the parkway has ceased, contractors are suing Georgia DOT for damages, and the eventual outcome remains unclear. Meanwhile, construction of the Carter Library complex is proceeding.

BARRIERS TO PUBLIC PARTICIPATION

The argument can perhaps be made that there was never any real opportunity for productive discourse between the public and parkway proponents. In a real sense, Georgia DOT's action decades ago to acquire and clear the land, the divisive struggle that ensued, and the years of dispute over the future of the land have all tended to harden positions and stifle meaningful dialogue. By examining such an extreme example, however, we can perhaps begin to appreciate and understand the truly complex series of obstacles that complicate public involvement in land-use planning and decision making. At least five can be noted in the Atlanta situation.

Public Participation vs. Public Disclosure

The term "public participation" defies definition, at least in a way that meets with agreement from both policy makers and citizens. Citizens interpret the concept to mean being invited to sit at the planning table, to fully participate, and to be involved in weighing the merits of a particular project and its alternatives. On the other hand, agencies—at least if their actions are any indication—frequently seem to confuse public participation with public disclosure. Through environmental impact statements and public meetings, the public is provided detailed technical information and justifications for an agency's proposed action but is forced into the posture of reacting to a decision rather than participating in it.

Such was clearly the case in Atlanta. Georgia DOT never even made a pretense that the fundamental question of whether the parkway was necessary should be subject to public debate. By arguing that its hands were tied by legal requirements for disposition of the right-of-way, Georgia DOT from the very start presented the highway as a fait accompli. It is therefore hardly surprising that the issue became so fraught with contention. Georgia DOT's exhaustive effort to "disclose" to the public its plans for the parkway merely added fuel to the fire.

Point vs. Counterpoint: The Weakness of Microanalysis

When trying to impose some order on such a huge volume of public comment as that received on the parkway case, there is a natural tendency for a project agency to separate all of the varied comments into discrete elements: "Access to my driveway will be cut off," "My street will become a dead end," "Our tennis courts will be lost," etc. Once isolated from the corpus of comments, a response to each very specific issue can then be fashioned. This process is continued until all of the specific issues are addressed. If regarded as an end in itself rather than a means to an end, such microanalysis, however, can lead to a serious distortion of the public record. An agency, either wittingly or otherwise, uses this analysis technique as a way of not coming to grips with the cumulative impacts of the full body of comments. Thus Georgia DOT offered a volume of responses to particular and very specific issues, but never confronted the overwhelming opposition to the project clearly apparent from the collective comments of the public.

Technical Immutability vs. the Laymen

As our society has become more and more specialized, the gulf separating the technical expert from the public has grown larger. Specialization, while a natural outgrowth of technology, has led in some ways to professional isolation; knowledge is compartmentalized and colleagues speak only among themselves in a language foreign to the uninitiated. When this tendency is carried to an extreme, technical experts may appear to believe that their professional judgments are beyond informed public understanding and immune to public criticism. In such a climate, constructive public discourse is overwhelmed by technically superior firepower.

Again, the parkway case is illustrative. Even though neighborhood spokespersons repeatedly argued that filtering traffic on local streets was not perceived as a major problem, Georgia DOT offered a litany of statistics and traffic projections to insist that it was a problem that demanded a solution. Citizen suggestions that transportation needs could be met by a series of alternative measures such as selected intersection improvements and signalization, or that the parkway could be scaled back in design, were dismissed as naive responses to complex engineering and transportation requirements. While citizens acknowledged that Georgia DOT was technically more qualified to address the issues, many people believed the agency used its technical superiority as an excuse to avoid looking beyond the numbers and formulas to gain an understanding of the neighborhoods' point of view.

The Public as Phantom

In the political process the public is most easily perceived as the voter: one person, one vote. Only in those rare instances in which a land-use issue is put to the vote is it possible for public input to be so directly expressed. In most land-use decisions, deciphering both public opinions and "public opinion" is far more problematic. Quantitative analysis must invariably yield to subjective evaluations, a fact that may account for why those most accustomed to solving problems with engineering methods are often uncomfortable with public participation. To be of any real value, public comment cannot be considered in a vacuum nor—as was the case in Atlanta—should it be reduced to "us versus them" or "pro versus con."

Why did neighborhood residents feel so strongly in their opposition? Were unstated agendas at work? These and similar questions must be asked in order for decision makers to fully understand the public response. Such subjective evaluations, however, are seldom offered for public scrutiny, although it is apparent to interested observers that they are taking place. Thus, it is no wonder that the public is highly suspicious of the criteria being used to make these judgments, and comes to believe that the application of those criteria is self-serving.

Pursuit of Self-Fulfillment vs. the Public Good

"How," planners ask, "can we expect to achieve consensus in a public forum when citizens are motivated by personal agenda and not the welfare of the community at large for which we are accountable?" How indeed do we account for the adversarial nature of most public participation? Zane Miller, an historian who has examined the changing concepts of community and civic activism in Cincinnati, sees such conflict inherent in current attitudes that equate the public good with the welfare of individuals in pursuit of their own self-interests. Articulating the frustration felt by many public policy makers, and no doubt Georgia DOT, he writes:

Because self-fulfillment is a personal and private matter, almost any general action by a government can be construed as inhibiting the quest for self-realization by some persons or groups. As a result, civic activism is increasingly embodied in negative or oppositional rather than constructive goals.

This leads us toward a . . . situation where it is easier to mobilize opposition to policies and programs than it is to create and implement them. It also makes any consensus about sacrifice difficult to achieve, since programs conceived in the public interest will almost always impose costs and sacrifices upon someone. In effect, our unacknowledged pursuit of a community of liberated individuals blurs into indistinction the concept of public good (Miller, 1983).

Such a criticism has frequently been lodged against those opposing "public improvement" projects. This dichotomy of interests tends to create an atmosphere of hostility and misunderstanding, making any partnership between the government and the public difficult to achieve. Certainly Georgia DOT believed its opponents were indifferent to the transportation needs of the region. However, it can also be argued that, by its dogmatic insistence on pursuing the parkway in the face of such strong neighborhood sentiment against it, Georgia DOT was blind to equally legitimate goals of maintaining quality neighborhoods. Herein lies the danger. Frustrated by the belief that critics are motivated only by self-interests, an agency is likely to dismiss public input outright and assume that it knows best where the public good lies.

CONCLUSION

In the final analysis, only two requirements are essential for over-coming these barriers and making public participation an effective component of land-use decision making. First, policy makers, through actions rather than words, have to convince citizens that they will be involved in setting the planning agenda and not just reacting to it. It has been shown that, when public participation is an integral part of early planning, it can be an extremely positive force in solving problems. In a recent survey of neighborhood planning programs throughout the country (Rohe and Gates, 1985), found that such approaches to local planning led to consensus building and have had the added advantage of generating a greater sense of community solidarity and cohesiveness. Governments at the local level need to promote such citizen-based programs for planning, and state and federal agencies should open direct channels of communication to such groups in their planning processes.

Second, when disputes arise, policy makers must act to assure citizens that such conflicts will be addressed openly and that reasonable attempts will be made to resolve such differences through negotiation. Certainly, one of the most encouraging developments in recent years has been the growing success of environmental dispute resolution. Dispute resolution has demonstrated that solutions to problems resulting from competing land-use desires are only possible when people are willing to listen to both sides of an issue. Rather than steering blindly against the headwinds of public opposition, and thus inviting lengthy and costly litigation, agencies need to adopt techniques of joint problem solving, mediation, and dispute resolution as a more constructive and responsible means of doing what in fact is, and should be, the public's business.

Bibliography

Advisory Council on Historic Preservation. 1984. "Executive Director's Report: Presidential Parkway, Atlanta, Georgia." Washington, D.C. (January) Mimeo.

Fitch, James Marston. 1982. *Historic Preservation: Curatorial Management of the Built Environment*. New York: McGraw-Hill.

Levy-Leboyer, Claude. 1982. *Psychology and Environment*. Translated by David Canter and Ian Griffiths. Beverly Hills, CA: Sage.

Miller, Zane L. 1983. "History and the Politics of Community Change in Cincinnati." *The Public Historian* 5 (Fall): 17–35.

Raiffa, Howard. 1982. *The Art and Science of Negotiations*. Cambridge: Harvard University Press.

Rohe, William M., and Lauren B. Gates. 1985. *Planning with Neighborhoods*. Chapel Hill: University of North Carolina Press.

Special Committee on Historic Preservation, United States Conference of Mayors. 1966. *With Heritage So Rich*. New York: Random House.

U.S. Department of Transportation, Federal Highway Administration, and Georgia Department of Transportation. 1985. "Addendum to Section 4(f) Statement, Georgia Project M–9152(2), Presidential Parkway, Fulton/DeKalb Counties, Georgia" (Atlanta).

———. 1984. "Final Environmental Impact Statement, Georgia Project M–9152(2), Presidential Parkway, Fulton/DeKalb Counties, Georgia" (Atlanta).

———. 1983. "Draft Environmental Impact Statement, Georgia Project M–9152(2), Presidential Parkway, Fulton/DeKalb Counties, Georgia" (Atlanta).

9

ALTERNATIVE CONFLICT MANAGEMENT TECHNIQUES IN LAND-USE DECISIONS: SANIBEL ISLAND CASE STUDY

Jerome Delli Priscoli

ABSTRACT

This chapter describes how alternative dispute resolution (ADR) techniques can be applied to potentially controversial land-use decisions. The case involves wetland use on Sanibel Island, Florida. The technique was to use a general permit, under the Section 404 authority, to focus debate, to generate alternatives, and to reach agreement among interested and affected parties on how to develop Sanibel's wetlands. The chapter describes how the federal government used its authority to encourage those who were closest to the land use to come to an agreement on the specification of a general permit. This agreement became the permit which was unchallenged for its five-year life. The chapter portrays a model of intergovernmental relations where the federal government consciously became facilitator to rather than dictator of policy.

Key Words: U.S. Army Corps of Engineers, Section 404 permitting, Comprehensive Land Use Plan, Sanibel plan, public involvement, land use planning, planning negotiations

INTRODUCTION

How will land be used? By whom? Who will pay? Who will benefit? Who owns the land? Who has the right to determine the use of land? Does private ownership mean unconstrained use? If the answers are no then what are the limits for the common good? What is the common good? Who determines it—a group of screaming environmentalists, or gray bureaucrats? Why should I think that a bureaucrat who hasn't even been elected, should determine what I do with my land? But do individuals deciding by self-interests lead to the general good? Can we avoid the tragedy of the commons, but still preserve freedom of individual action? Land-use decisions have been, and are, the frequent battlegrounds for answering such fundamental questions.

How often have you heard it said that the goverment is not supposed to be in the national land-use planning business? Nevertheless, various agencies of the federal government are charged to protect national interests in areas such as environment which imply certain land uses. Everybody wants "rational" land use, but nobody seems to want a big brother planning. Everybody has a different view of "rationality."

BACKGROUND

This chapter describes how such questions were addressed in one case study involving a general permit for wetland fill on Sanibel Island, Florida. First it examines background, theory, and concepts behind the general permitting approach. It then describes issues, actors, and interests; the workshop process used to develop a consensus among parties of conflict; the costs and benefits of the approach; and the conclusions.

Land use is thought to be primarily a localized decision. However, under Section 404 of the 1972 Water Pollution Control Act, the U.S. Army Corps of Engineers was given responsibilities for issuing permits for construction in wetlands across the United States. Together with its older Section 10 authority for issuing permits in navigable waters, the Corps now issues around 18,000 permits a year. Most of these permits are noncontroversial, but many of them do generate controversy.

Under Section 404, the Corps grants individual permits for most forms of construction activities such as diking and filling land which take place in wetlands. Generally individual permits are granted, but the law also allows Corps district engineers to issue general permits when the activities that would be conducted are similar and do not produce negative cumulative impacts. The following case is a study of how one general permit was used to encourage agreement among usually conflicting parties over answers to questions such as those already mentioned.

In 1978, the district engineer of the Jacksonville District decided that the general permit could be a way to increase efficiency of the permitting process, to decrease the amount of public funds expended, to decrease the probability of court cases, and to protect the wetlands as required in the law. He liked the general permit because it offered economy in processing, provided environmental safeguards up-front, and defined in advance what an applicant can do.

Permit applicant believed that uncertainty due to waiting was a major problem. Only after a completed application had been submitted and reviewed did the applicant learn whether the proposed action was acceptable. On the other hand, a general permit defined in advance the acceptable actions. It also clearly stated the conditions by which the applicant could abide, which should include stringent environmental protection. Now the nature of these conditions is very important because environmentalists typically fear that the general permit could be a carte blanche for construction or a return to the days of few constraints.

On Sanibel, the Corps decided to do something different. Rather than writing the general permit inhouse, the Corps suggested that the interested parties—who were often in conflict—come together to write the specifications for a general permit. In 1980 this was a revolutionary idea and remains so even with further successful applications of this approach (Delli Priscoli, 1987).

The Corps said, in essence, to the environmental community, citizens, potential contractors, other federal agencies, and state and local agencies that if you can agree to the specifications of a permit, within the broad general outlines of Section 404, the Corps would simply confirm that agreement and call the agreement a general permit. That is, the general permit would become an "up-front" agreement with the force of the Corps authority. In this way, the Corps moved beyond a role of technical reviewer to that of facilitator of consensus among local land users. That was the innovative idea. The Corps was not doing the land-use planning for Sanibel Island. Rather, the Corps was saying to those who determine land use on the island, "If you can agree among yourselves, then we will affirm and honor that agreement." In effect, the Corps was using its authority as a carrot to encourage local vested interests to do what they rarely do, which is to agree on a land-use plan!

From the beginning, this approach encountered resistance. For example, one Corps executive said that it couldn't be done because the information received in using this proposed workshop process would not be valid in court. The district engineer's response was that the reasoning behind achieving a general permit in this way was to stay out of court and to reduce costs to the taxpayer!

Despite varied resistance, the District proceeded with a series of four workshops which included the U.S. Fish and Wildlife Service, the U.S. Environmental Protection Agency, Florida Department of Environmental Regulation, other state government departments, county government departments, local planning commissions, city managers, city council members, special interest groups such as the vegetation committees, absentee and resident landowner committees, development corporations, the Audubon society, and others. These parties agreed and the resultant general permit has functioned for its expected five years. It worked because the parties of conflict owned it and because the Corps adopted more than a traditional technical review or advocate role and actively facilitated the agreement.

ACTORS, ISSUES, INTERESTS, AND POSITION

Considerable thought went into selecting Sanibel Island as the place to test this general-permit approach. The factors that went into the selection of Sanibel Island were:

1. The interior wetlands of the islands are substantially similar, so that overall standards could be reasonably applied.

2. If the special conditions are properly applied, the total cumulative impacts are expected to be minimal.

3. The District had received six to eight permit applications per year. The annual cost of processing these permits justified the initial costs of the ADR process in developing a general permit.

4. Sanibel Island is incorporated as a city and has developed a comprehensive land-use plan. This plan, which is used as the basis for all land-use planning and zoning on the island, has received national recognition as one of the first and finest attempts to relate growth to ecological limits. This plan would also be relied upon substantially in developing the conditions for a general permit.

5. The citizens of Sanibel Island are active in local affairs, responsive to new ideas, and environmentally sensitive. Some interest in a general permit had already been expressed by city officials.

Sanibel's new city government immediately issued a moratorium on new building permits and began drawing a new policy for growth. A planning organization and a law firm were engaged by the city to provide professional assistance, while an environmental firm was added to this team by the Island's Conservation Foundation. The efforts were directed toward devising, in Merle Lefkoff's words, " ... a strategy for conserving (the island's) threatened land and water resources, its beaches and mangroves, its drinking water and wildlife—in a word, its remarkable quality of life" (Delli Priscoli et al., 1983). In July 1976, having received the work of its consultants, known as the Comprehensive Land Use Plan (CLUP), the city approved the ordinances necessary to implement the plan. At the same time, the moratorium on building permits was lifted.

The Sanibel plan sought to balance the protection of the natural resources with a reasonable level of development. It established five directions for its work: it set a population limit consistent with natural limits; it distributed this population on the basis of the "carrying capacity" of the natural systems; it established a set of performance standards for all development; it developed a plan for the restoration of past ecologic damage; and it provided for a continuing public participation process. The CLUP has achieved national recognition as one of the first attempts to relate growth to ecological limits.

As a result of the restrictions, many properties which were purchased for sizeable developments were zoned to permit only minimal use. A few owners took their grievances to court over the down-zoning of their property. In one case, a developer owning 415 acres at the western end of the island had planned to build 1,600 units. Under CLUP, the land could be utilized for only 50 units. The developer claimed that the property was taken without just compensation and without due process.

The other common CLUP-related complaints concerned the time required to gain approval of development permits. The newness of the city government and the unique and untried nature of the Sanibel plan created processing problems and delays in the city. In addition, until this approach, the Corps relied exclusively upon individual permits, with each request for dredging or filling in the wetlands being reviewed and evaluated on an individual basis. The time-consuming processing instigated the current interest in the general permit.

The mayor and other city officials showed an interest in the general permit, in part because it might speed up the permitting process and reduce criticism of the city's CLUP. The city government was dominated by environmentalists who were certainly wary of the Corps of Engineers and the development of a permit through a public involvement process which seemed to circumvent the usual political process. The position of the city, despite early suspicion, was cooperative and positive, and the mayor and city planner participated directly in the workshops to insure that special conditions would be compatible with the CLUP.

Developers were interested in an acceptable and easily understood permitting process. They believed that a general permit would speed up permitting, which had been rife with delays in the past. Special conditions for fill activities with everyone agreed upon and understood would also work to their advantage. On the other hand, they were concerned that environmental interests on the island would dominate the workshops. Developers were skeptical about a public involvement process that did not signal political behind the scenes "business as usual." While officially supporting the workshops and a general permit, few developers participated directly in the process.

Environmentalists, including representatives of environmental groups as well as island residents unaffiliated with an organization, historically mistrusted the Corps. This mistrust was based on their negative perception of the Corps' flood control dams and structures. Their interests would not be served by a permitting process which speeded up permitting to the detriment of the environment. At the same time, the absence of a detailed set of criteria for the granting of permits was working to their disadvantage. Many developers and homeowners were proceeding to build structures without obtaining the necessary permits. So environmentalists shared with developers an interest in a permitting process that carefully spelled out special conditions for construction activities. They also shared an interest with the city in making sure that the special conditions in the general permit did not subvert the CLUP requirements. Environmentalists split their position at the beginning of the workshops. Some were adamantly opposed to a general permit on principle and others were willing to try developing adequate special conditions.

Issues Addressed in Special Conditions

The following issues were among those discussed during the Sanibel workshops:

1. Periodic inspections by Corps personnel of fill activities
2. Erosion problems created by a rise in elevation substantially above existing grade
3. "Grandfathering" and the general permit
4. Buffer zones around wetland preserves
5. Geographic boundaries of the general permit
6. Concurrent processing on the federal, state and local levels
7. Siltation problems created by fills too close to rivers or other water bodies
8. Stabilization of slopes through active revegetation programs
9. The need to avoid revegetation with exotic or aggressive species
10. Protection of fish, wildlife, and natural environmental values
11. Protection of mangroves
12. Protection of National Register historic properties

Process and Outcome

A team of four consultants assisted the Corps in the design, implementation, and evaluation of the workshop process. They also studied the history of land-use planning on the island, paying particularly close attention to Sanibel's historic CLUP. The consultants also reviewed the Corps' jurisdiction and responsibilities where the general permit was concerned. These activities helped the district engineer outline his goals and objectives. Since the process was new, an independent evaluator was commissioned to do a real-time evaluation of the process.

A Corps staffer was assigned to be a liaison with the consultants and a general administrative troubleshooter. He assembled a mailing list for preworkshop information dissemination. It was essential to the success of the process that the people attending the workshops represent an equitable distribution of interests.

The last task before the first workshop was to design and to administer a series of interviews with identified community influentials on Sanibel. Both a short, structured interview and a longer, more informal interview were used to elicit comments on potentially important issues from individuals who were likely to be important actors in the process. Interviewers included persons from the Jacksonville District office of the Corps, local officials, city planners, and leaders of the environmental community.

The district office selected eight persons from their staff to be workshop facilitators. The Corps' Institute for Water Resources (IWR) performed the impossible. In only six hours on the day before the first workshop, they turned eight apprehensive "raw recruits" into skilled and assured facilitators. This was not enough time to brief the Corps staff on the history of the island and the likely actors in the process, as well as teaching the "tricks of the trade" of the trained facilitator. They drew strength from each other and were able to exchange facilitator and recorder roles; they helped to ease the strain of playing one role only and this enabled them to test a variety of skills.

As Corps personnel who are in the field and in contact with the public, the facilitators played the most important role in the process. They had a dual mission: to gain new skills from "on-the-job training" with live citizens in a live situation and to help the citizens reach consensus on the necessary criteria for a general permit. Their job was to keep the group process moving, without imposing their own values, judgments, or official expertise—a very difficult task.

The consultant's job was to prepare the facilitators for the group process as carefully as possible, to allay their fears and insecurities by providing them with the basic process tools of good communication. But the key to the successful training of the Corps staff was a training situation quite different from the traditional, sterile classroom techniques. They learned where the rubber meets the road. The facilitators learned "jointly" with the workshop participants how to communicate, interact, moderate conflict, and produce a product.

The first workshop draw about 50 people, not a disappointing crowd for a full-day workshop held midweek on a hot summer day. The Corps stationed a receptionist at the door of the meeting room to log participants in and to give them name tags with a number one to six. These numbers were randomly assigned and indicated the six small "break-out" groups anticipated during late-morning. This random assignment prevented groups of friends who arrived together from forming their own groups.

The district engineer began the morning with a briefing session which explained the Corps' jurisdiction over the wetlands, the general permitting process, and the new process in which the citizens were soon to participate. An important part of the colonel's presentation was his sincere assurances to the assembled citizens: no decision on the issuance of a general permit had been made, nor would it be made until after the series of workshops had been completed and until after the public comments were received in response to the public notice; the district engineer would accept or reject in total the consensus of workshop participants as to the language of the special conditions under the general permit; and all views would have ample time to be aired and taken into consideration.

Several citizens announced that they were suspicious of the proceedings and even more suspicious of the effect that a general permit would have on Sanibel's ecology. The facilitators were introduced by the district engineer. Each led his or her group to a small meeting room which was already equipped with the essential props for the group discussion: an easel, on which there was placed ample newsprint; several magic markers; and adhesive tape with which to tack a record of the discussion on the surrounding walls for everyone to see. After appropriate ice-breaking, the facilitator then explained that the "product" of the first workshop was to be a set of tear sheets that would document the group's "scoping" of all possible issues which should be considered in the general permit. The group was then asked to select from among themselves a "reporter" to report the group's deliberations to a meeting of the whole at the end of the day.

When participants returned to the large meeting at 3:00 P.M., the results were remarkable. As the group reporters delivered their synopses it became clear that all groups agreed upon basic problems to be solved, although each group managed to "scope" at least a few issues that were overlooked by the others. The unsolicited testimony of several participants was even more remarkable. The process successfully dampened their suspicions about what the Corps might be up to. The gentleman who had announced his adamant opposition to a general permit rose before the whole group and admitted that his earlier opposition was beginning to dissipate.

The colonel thanked everyone for coming and asked the citizens to indicate before they left whether they would be continuing as participants in the other scheduled workshops. Also, the group was asked to add a short note about whether their expectations were met. This note was added to earlier statements of their purpose for participating and of their expectations. The results of these first evaluations were overwhelmingly favorable.

The Corps and its consultants undertook three tasks in preparation for the next workshop: (1) they synthesized and refined the comments made by the citizens in their small group sessions, categorizing the range of problems into four main issue areas; (2) they prepared a summary of the first workshop proceedings and designed "task assignments" for the small groups which would be assembling at the second workshop; and (3) they prepared a short report of the process problems and successes encountered at the first workshop, making recommendations for the conduct of the next meeting. This work formed the basis for the second mailing to citizen participants prior to the second workshop. The report enabled them to recap the issues and start thinking about the issues for the next meeting.

At the second workshop, the Corps wanted individuals to focus on their special concerns and to use their expertise in one special area. Participants were asked to read the materials mailed ahead of time and to indicate the issue groups to which they wanted to be assigned. No random assignments of groups were made at the second workshop. The mailing for the second workshop invited those who had indicated that they wished to be kept informed, in addition to the state and local lists. This second workshop produced a refinement of numerous issues scoped at the first meeting and began the detailed work of writing language for the special conditions for the general permit.

The third workshop was crucial because the special conditions had to be written at that time so the larger community might have a final opportunity at the fourth and final workshop to respond to the language of the special conditions. Once again, the Corps returned to a format where each small group addressed all issues and language under consideration. Consensus was reached smoothly by the end of the day, and the final language was produced.

Because we expected a lower turnout than at the initial meeting, the fourth workshop was only a half-day session. Its purpose was to wrap up loose ends. In case citizens with no prior involvement showed up at this last workshop, we asked several citizens who had emerged as leaders within their work groups to serve as a panel to answer questions from the floor. Since the citizens themselves had developed the special conditions, they should be the ones to explain their work before their friends and neighbors. We thought it ill-advised to place the Corps in a defensive posture at this late stage in the game.

The give-and-take between panelists and the audience was easy and informal. The district engineer answered the tough procedural questions that the citizens could not address. The meeting produced a few minor changes in the language of the special conditions and a lot of backpatting. The colonel was eloquent in his congratulations to the community for their hard work. The community was equally delighted with the good faith shown by the Corps.

The public notice—or "Green Sheet," as it's known in the district—was sent out, incorporating the language of the special conditions developed at the workshops. With trepidation all awaited the results of the comment period. Only five letters were received. One minor problem with the language of the special conditions appeared dealing with the fill elevation in order to accommodate septic tanks. The language was changed slightly for the final permit, after concurrence from the workshop participants (who were polled by the Corps) and the Corps. The Corps also began to negotiate with the City of Sanibel on how to cooperate in administering the general permit.

WHAT WAS LEARNED?

As mentioned, two evaluations were commissioned. An outside party studied the attitudes and perceptions of all participants as the process emerged. This was a unique real-time evaluation. Such evaluation is rare in most of government policy programs and extremely rare in public involvement and conflict management. The Corps' managers also did an internal cost-benefit analysis of the process.

These evaluations are interesting. They documented a fundamental attitude shift of participants. Of those whose attitude toward the permit changed as a result of the workshop, 72 percent changed from neutral to positive, 14 percent from negative to positive, and 7 percent from negative to neutral. In addition, all participants had positive attitudes toward the workshops. The data showed that citizens considered that workshops were conducive to a constructive dialogue, and that they gained understanding of how permitting processes worked. What they learned made them less apprehensive about speeding up the permitting process.

The evaluation also indicated that the image of the Corps was enhanced by the process. The Corps was able to get an indication of citizen desires about protection of wetlands; the Corps shared its decision-making authority with citizens; a general permit did issue; the Corps and local government would share enforcement responsibilities; and Corps personnel were trained in being neutral workshops facilitators. Also, the need for a formalized public hearing on the permit was eliminated.

Similarly, the goals of the environmentalists were also achieved. Wetlands would be protected by the general permit conditions; citizens did have an opportunity to write their permit conditions; and certainty about development constraints had been provided to the environmentalists, landowners, and public officials in Sanibel.

Although Sanibel was successful a question to be considered is why did the people agree, and can it work in other places? In general, people agreed because the general permit itself reduced uncertainty. They agreed to the process because of the trust relationship that was built. Environmentalists believed that uncertainty was reduced and that they would be better able to program their scarce resources for battles in other areas. Developers saw time as money and the certainty achieved with the permit reduced the probability that they would have to lose money in the future.

Among those factors contributing to the success of the process were the following:

1. Careful preliminary data collection gave planners a good handle on likely actors, issues, and political environment

2. Discussions with individuals most likely to be antagonistic were held prior to the workshops

3. The "rules of the game" were universally agreed upon and understood at the outset of the process; participants were not "pushed" into taking action because sufficient time was allotted to the process

4. Products were summarized after each workshop and mailed to participants prior to the next workshop

5. Workshop times and locations were set in order to maximize participation

6. The facilitators from the Corps received professional facilitator training

7. Corps personnel responded quickly to any and all requests for information

There are, however, a number of other factors with this case that should be considered. They include, but are not limited to, the following:

1. The political climate, while not favorable initially to the general permit, was favorable to the discussion of permitting on the island

2. The timing of the participation was good

3. The facilitation role adopted by the Corps was crucial

4. The Corps used consultants, in particular a trusted environmental consultant, to support the process and to discuss the process and to assure its validity before it began

5. A credible range and variety of interests were represented at the workshops

6. Information was readily made available to participants

7. The expectations of Corps personnel and other participants were closely aligned largely due to the early training of Corps participants before the process started

8. Acceptance of the process and product occurred largely because ownership of what became a success was shared among the Corps and participants

9. Attitudinal changes of participants occurred

10. The Sanibel area had clear geographic boundaries, a history of land-use planning, and a sophisticated population who were literate in environmental concerns

11. Sanibel had the CLUP, and intermediaries who could engender trust

12. Finally, Sanibel had a short history of two previous failed efforts

WHAT ARE THE ALTERNATIVES?

There are alternatives to approaches such as the Sanibel approach. The Corps could have proceeded on a permit-by-permit basis. This would have meant increased litigation costs and would have placed a premium on the advocacy process. The Corps could also have done a general area analytical or environmental study. Such studies highlight major dimensions of environmental sensitivity which are then considered on a case-by-case basis by permit processors. While useful, the approach still falls short of a general permit. They lack teeth and do not have the force of regulation. One reason Sanibel worked was that the carrots were real. Participation had a tangible benefit—namely direct input to a document with teeth that would be used if agreement occurred. Finally, I suppose some form of regional federal land-use planning could be instituted. However, this has not really been achieved in the past and its utility might be questionable.

Another question frequently asked is whether it was technically valid? Agreement does not necessarily mean "correctness." Just because the parties of interest agreed does not mean that the general permit was technically correct. This criticism gets into a deeper discussion of where one discovers the truth in scientific facts. Let me leave this by saying that the best environmental expertise in the area, along with engineering expertise, all had strong feelings on what was appropriate. Out of the mixing and matching of these points of view a consensus developed. Actually, the professional engineering staff of the Corps believed that the wording of the general permit was better, technically, than anything they had come up with or proposed in the past.

Finally, as others have discussed elsewhere, encouraging participation of local people often increases and enhances staff capacity, because the citizens are not only motivated but frequently they possess great expertise. Therefore, consensus in this case, and in many others, can also enhance the technical aspects of decisions.

CONCLUSIONS

So what can we say about land-use planning and conflict management based on this one case? First, this process cannot be used everywhere. However, its success and "real-time" documentation deserve a wider audience and study. The case raises a number of important issues on how to approach the fundamental problem of land use. Can we get sufficient consensus so that we may act? The first lesson we learned was that government, in this case the Corps, acted as a facilitator, not just a technical reviewer or a "dictator" of specific decisions. The use of the federal government programs to facilitate could be a key to land-use decisions. As facilitator to rather than dictator of the agreement, the federal government could hold out its carrots—such as permits and grant money—for demonstrable public consensus among those responsible for the land use. We should examine the role of government as facilitator rather than simply as technical expert, especially in this era of federal austerity.

We also learned that good process can mean good efficiency which essentially means good government. Time, money, and other burdens on the public—both environmentalists and developers—were reduced while at the same time protecting the environment and enhancing the quality of decisions.

Consensus building, participation, and conflict management do not mean bad technical decisions. In fact, they can mean enhanced technical decisions.

The key to building consensus is to develop a sense of shared ownership in the process by which decisions are reached as well as in the decisions themselves. It is to bring the experience of community to interested, affected, and often antagonistic people.

NOTES

Many people were involved with Sanibel. This article paraphrases articles on this case done by Judy Roesner, Merle Lefkoff, Paul Munch, and Jerome Delli Priscoli, all appearing in *Public Involvement Techniques: A Reader of Ten Years Experience at the Institute for Water Resources*, IWR Research Report 82-R1 (May 1983), Ft. Belvoir, VA.

Bibliography

Comprehensive Land Use Plan (Sanibel Island, Fla.)

Delli Priscoli, Jerome. 1987. "Conflict Resolution in Water Resources: Two Cases of Using Facilitation and Mediation to Write Section 404 General Permits." Paper presented at the annual conference of ASCE-Water Resources Planning and Management Division, Kansas City, March 16.

Delli Priscoli, Jerome et al. 1983. *Public Involvement Techniques: A Reader of Ten Years Experience at the Institute for Water Resources*. May, Ft. Belvoir, VA.

Fisher, R., and W. Ury. 1981. *Getting to Yes*. Boston: Houghton Mifflin.

Manks, J. B. et al. *Dispute Resolution in America: Process in Evolution*. 1984. Washington, D.C.: National Institute for Dispute Resolution.

Pneuman, R. W., and M. E. Bruehl. 1982. *Managing Conflict*. Englewood Cliffs, NJ: Prentice-Hall.

U.S. Army Corp of Engineers. "Section 404, General Permit 1980, Sanibel Island." Jacksonville District, Jacksonville, FL.

Wehr, Paul. 1979. *Conflict Regulation*. Boulder, CO: Westview Press.

10

POLICY IMPLICATIONS IN MANAGING PUBLIC LANDS

Rochelle L. Stanfield

ABSTRACT

After 200 years of misusing the land, we are discovering that there are no independent land-use decisions. The interconnections are global, such as the link between tropical deforestation and the "greenhouse effect," and local such as the impact of water projects on the ecology of adjacent lands. Government still tends to look at pollution control from the perspective of the various individual media, but attention to cross-media pollution and control is growing. The next step is to avoid creating the waste in the first place, but that is still far down the road.

Key Words: land use planning/management, pollution abatement, cross-media pollution, environmental consciousness, waste reduction/ management, land conservation

INTRODUCTION

Our use, overuse, and misuse of the land is catching up with us.

For 200 years we have stripped the land bare, built it up, drained it dry, filled it in, moved it around, polluted it with toxic materials, and even changed its internal chemistry. When we thought about the consequences of these actions, we generally looked at the immediate impact on surrounding areas.

Now we are discovering that there are no independent land-use decisions. Each river that is dammed, every forest that is cut down, and each swamp that is drained not only directly affects its immediate surroundings but also contributes to profound changes in regional, continental, and even global environmental conditions.

The consequences of decades of shortsighted land-use decisions are becoming increasingly apparent. On a global scale, deforestation is causing the loss of stratospheric ozone and the extinction of tropical species by the millions, in many cases before they are identified. Around the U.S., as a result of various public works projects designed to enhance land use as well as careless waste disposal and other misuses of the land, water tables are declining, groundwater is contaminated, soil is eroding, and there are questions about the continued productivity of the forests.

Even if we could, we are not going to stop our land-consuming, chemical-dependent civilization from irrevocably altering much of the environment. The challenge is to lengthen our perspectives: to discern the full consequences of each use of the land, to decide which impacts we will tolerate and which we cannot accept, to incorporate these decisions into enlightened plans for land use, and to garner the political will to implement these plans. As a society we are broadening our view. But in our typical democratic way, we have a very ad hoc, disorganized manner of incorporating this newfound understanding into land-use management.

IN THE SAME BOAT

The early conservationists intuitively understood the interconnectedness of nature. As John Muir, who founded the Sierra Club, put it nearly a century ago: "When we try to pick out anything by itself, we find it hitched to everything else in the universe."[1]

Satellite pictures of Spaceship Earth reinforced the image that "we are all in the same boat together" to pioneers of the renewed environmental movement in the early 1970s.

Now basic research findings in biology, chemistry, physics, and such new disciplines as biogeochemical cycles are transforming an ethical principle and political watchword into hard science. Researchers are finding links between tropical deforestation and the "greenhouse effect" that is raising global temperatures, for example, and between tiny forest creatures such as the tree vole and the ability of the forests to regenerate themselves.

The data are growing. The Hubbard Brook Experimental Research Station in New Hampshire's White Mountain National Forest, for example, conducted controlled experiments that showed forests lose more nutrients when clear-cut than when other forms of timbering are used.[2] But the management of land use does not lend itself to controlled experiments, and the results of the kind of research conducted on complex systems are rarely unequivocal.

Many scientists rely on mathematical models of different processes within the systems, but models have drawbacks. "If there are incorrect specifications or if the model is too simplified, you don't get the complete picture. You can't get a detailed model of an ecosystem, for example, because there are parts of it we don't know about yet," explained one government researcher.[3] So scientists try to correlate cause and effect from multiple observations of similar phenomena. "The idea is to make so many correlations that no rational person could deny the connection—like smoking and cancer," explained another researcher.[4]

The incredible complexity of these systems prolongs the data-gathering process which, in turn, complicates and confuses the decision-making process, perhaps until it is too late to avert the consequences.

The sensitivity of government, industry, and society as a whole to these interconnections is growing, however, and environmental issues are beginning to be viewed from a broader perspective. While specific offices within the U.S. Environmental Protection Agency (EPA) continue to attack the individual concerns of air, water, and solid waste pollution, for example, the agency as a whole is beginning to look at cross-media pollution, the migration of pollutants from one medium to another such as buried smokestack sludge contaminating the groundwater. The Congressional Office of Technology Assessment calculates that 99 percent of the money government devotes to dealing with waste focuses on its disposal (U.S. Cong., OTA, 1986, p. 16). But increasing attention is being directed to preventing the generation of waste in the first place. Conservationists continue to fight to save a spectacular vista or unusual natural phenomenon, but more and more they are trying to protect whole ecosystems.

CROSS-MEDIA POLLUTION

Nowhere is the interconnectedness of the environment demonstrated more dramatically than in the problem of cross-media pollution, which has vastly complicated land-use planning.

Environmental engineers of the late 1960s and early 1970s who tackled the smoky haze cloaking most cities, the turgid gunk clogging the waterways, and the putrid smell arising from landfills generally confined their control strategies to removing pollutants from a single medium. But the pollutants scrubbed from the air or burned out of the water at sewage treatment plants simply turned up in other parts of the environment. Emissions from a Philadelphia sewage treatment plant were found to be the major air polluter in the area. Swamps and riverbanks once made popular landfill sites. Leaking contaminants have turned them into Superfund toxic waste cleanup sites.

Recognizing the cross-media problem, no mean feat in itself, is much easier than dealing with it. Controlling pollution in a single medium is a comparatively straightforward engineering task; considering the total environmental impact of each control method and effectively managing environmental systems is a much more complicated undertaking. The EPA's difficulty in drawing up regulations to implement provisions of the 1984 Resource Conservation and Recovery Act amendments that ban untreated waste from sanitary landfills is one illustration.

The best way to avoid the consequences of cross-media pollution is to avoid the generation of pollution in the first place. Not only is waste prevention a logical environmental step, it generally saves the polluter money. The slow pace of its implementation thus confounds many of its advocates.

WASTE REDUCTION

"Waste reduction is an economically sensible response to what many people see as a hazardous waste crisis," begins a recent Office of Technology Assessment report on the subject (U.S. Cong., OTA, 1986, p. 3). In 1985, the 40 companies that participated in the North Carolina state pollution prevention program saved a total of $12 million (Schecter 1986). Exxon Corporation's chemical plant in New Jersey found that the floating roofs it installed on chemical tanks to comply with state air pollution regulations saved substantially more money than the cost of the roofs. Exxon has since installed similar roofs on plants in states where they are not required (Sarokin et al., 1985).

Despite the logic of pollution prevention, the notion is difficult to implant in polluters because it requires a totally different approach to conducting business. For thousands of years, no one questioned the action of throwing out waste, and land disposal was the cheapest method. Now the Resource Conservation and Recovery Act is dramatically increasing the cost of land disposal. So industry looks for another cheap method of disposal. Injecting wastes into deep wells appears the next cheapest method. While environmentalists worry about the consequences of deep-well injection, government regulations overseeing its use do not discourage it. A USS Chemicals Inc. chemical plant in Ohio decided to continue operating its deep-well disposal system, which costs $50,000 a year to keep up, rather than to prevent the generation of phenol wastes or to recycle them, because the company believed to do so would be more expensive and complicated (Sarokin et al., 1985).

"Waste reduction alternatives were seldom considered until circumstances virtually forced plants to review their waste management practices," concluded a survey of waste reduction in the organic chemical industry (ibid.). That report concludes that government regulations have been instrumental in achieving the waste reduction progress to date. That does not necessarily translate into the need for a new government regulatory program, however. The Office of Technology Assessment finds "it would be extraordinarily difficult for government to set and enforce waste reduction standards for a myriad of industrial processes," according to its report (U.S. Cong., OTA, 1986, p. 4).

The answer is changing the mindset of industry and the general public, along with government regulators, of "establishing a new waste reduction ethic," in the words of OTA (ibid., p. 40). That will take longer and require a far more subtle and innovative approach than fist-banging regulations.

The same is true with land conservation. An Ecosystems Preservation Act is probably not the answer, at least now, to the disappearance of forests, grasslands, and wetlands and the myriad wild species that inhabit them. Over the past 22 years, beginning with the 1964 Wilderness Act, Congress has put in place a set of laws that could be used to conserve these ecosystems, if they are enforced with a view to the long term.

Public concern is growing over the consequences of shortsighted land management, particularly worry about the greenhouse effect and the loss of biological diversity. The National Academy of Sciences and the Smithsonian Institution held a national forum on biodiversity in 1986. Organizers expressed amazed delight at the large turnout, which they attributed to this growing concern (Bastian, 1986).

Many fear that irreversible damage is taking place. Others disagree with the doomsayers. Some biologists are skeptical about the number of species that have become extinct, and other scientists note that natural events have destroyed entire categories of creatures, such as the dinosaurs.

In addition, some scientists who do not believe the damage is necessarily irreversible are working on building artificial wetlands. Others point out that not all the functions of a wetland can be restored since all the functions have not been identified yet.

Forests again cover the Appalachian Mountains and parts of New England that were denuded prior to the 1930s. But they are not the majestic groves of hardwoods that once grew there. Cattle graze on the scrubby plants that grow on parched western lands. But those lands will never return to the rich grassland ecosystem that was there prior to the damming of rivers and overgrazing of the land. And soil lost to erosion across the country will not come back for thousands of years, if ever.

Some scientists express concern for the future of the human race if misuse of the land continues. Others say humanity will probably find a way to survive. The real question is: Will our management of land use result in the kind of world in which we want to live?

NOTES

1. "When we try to pick out anything by itself, we find it hitched to everything else in the Universe," John Muir. Motto reprinted by Sierra Club.

2. Interviews received from researcher that had worked with The Hubbard Brook Experimental Research Station in New Hampshire's White Mountain National Forest.

3. Interviews received on background from federal researchers.

4. Ibid.

Bibliography

Bastian, Edward. 1986. International Activities Division of the Smithsonian Institution. Personal communication with author.

Sarokin, David J., Warren R. Muir, Catherine G. Miller, and Sebastian R. Sperber. 1985. *Cutting Chemical Wastes, What 29 Organic Chemical Plants are Doing to Reduce Hazardous Wastes.* New York: INFORM, p. 143.

Schecter, Roger N. 1986. Director of the Pollution Prevention Pays Program, N.C. Department of Natural Resources and Community Development. Personal communication with author.

U.S. Congress, Office of Technology Assessment. 1986. *Serious Reduction of Hazardous Waste: For Pollution Prevention and Industrial Efficiency.* OTA-ITE–317. Washington, D.C.: U.S. Government Printing Office, p. 16.

BACKGROUND READING

Brubaker, Sterling, ed. 1984. *Rethinking the Federal Lands*. Washington, D.C.: Resources for the Future.

Carstensen, Vernon, ed. 1962. *The Public Lands: Studies in the History of the Public Domain*. Madison, WI: University of Wisconsin Press.

Clawson, Marion. 1972. *America's Land and Its Uses*. Baltimore: Johns Hopkins Press.

Clawson, Marion. 1983. *The Federal Lands Revisited*. Washington, D.C.: Resources for the Future.

———. 1975. *Forests for Whom and for What?* Baltimore: Johns Hopkins University Press.

———. 1971. *The Bureau of Land Management*. New York: Praeger.

Clawson, Marion, and Jack L. Knetsch. 1966. *Economics of Outdoor Recreation*. Baltimore: Johns Hopkins University Press.

Commission on Fair Market Value Policy for Federal Coal Leasing. 1984. *Report*. Washington, D.C.: Commission on Fair Market Value Policy for Federal Coal Leasing.

Council on Environmental Quality. 1985. *Fifteenth Annual Report of the Council on Environmental Quality*. Washington, D.C.: Government Printing Office. (Annual reports for other years are also valuable.)

Culhane, Paul J. 1981. *Public Lands Politics—Interest Group Influence on the Forest Service and the Bureau of Land Management*. Washington, D.C.: Resources for the Future.

Dana, Samuel T., and Sally K. Fairfax. 1980. *Forest and Range Policy*, 2d ed. New York: McGraw-Hill.

Everhart, William C. 1972. *National Park Service*. New York: Praeger.

Fitch, James Marston. 1982. *Historic Preservation: Curatorial Management of the Built Environment*. New York: McGraw-Hill.

Foresta, Ronald A. 1985. *America's National Parks and Their Keepers*. Washington, D.C.: Resources for the Future.

Foss, Phillip. 1960. *Politics and Grass*. Seattle: University of Washington Press.

Fradkin, Philip L. 1984. *A River No More: The Colorado River and the West*. Tucson, AZ: University of Arizona Press.

Gates, Paul W. 1968. *History of Public Land Law Development*. Washington, D.C.: Government Printing Office.

Grey, G. W., and F. J. Deneke. 1978. *Urban Forestry*. New York: John Wiley and Sons.

Hall, C. A. S., and John W. Day, Jr. 1977. *Ecosystem Modeling in Theory and in Practice*. New York: John Wiley and Sons.

Hays, Samuel P. 1959. *Conservation and the Gospel of Efficiency*. Cambridge, MA: Harvard University Press.

Howe, Charles W. 1979. *Natural Resource Economics: Issues, Analysis, and Policy*. New York: John Wiley and Sons.

Ise, John. 1962. *Our National Park Policy—A Critical History*. Baltimore: Johns Hopkins Press.

Johnston, George M., and Peter M. Emerson, eds. 1984. *Public Lands and the U.S. Economy—Balancing Conservation and Development*. Boulder, CO: Westview Press.

LeMaster, Dennis C. 1984. *Decade of Change: The Remaking of Forest Service Statutory Authority During the 1970s*. Westport: Greenwood Press.

Leshy, John D. 1987. *The Mining Law: A Study in Perpetual Motion*. Washington, D.C.: Resources for the Future.

Manks, J. B. et al. 1984. *Dispute Resolution in America: Process in Evolution*. Washington, D.C.: National Institute for Dispute Resolution.

Nash, Roderick. 1973. *Wilderness and the American Mind*, rev. ed. New Haven, CT: Yale University Press.

Nelson, Robert H. 1983. *The Making of Federal Coal Policy*. Durham, NC: Duke University Press.

Odum, E. P. 1971. *Fundamentals of Ecology*, 3d ed. Philadelphia: W. B. Saunders Press.

Patric, William C. 1981. *Trust Land Administration in the Western States*. Denver: Public Lands Institute.

Pneuman, R. W., and M. E. Bruehl. 1982. *Managing Conflict*. Englewood Cliffs, NJ: Prentice-Hall.

Public Land Law Review Commission. 1970. *One Third of the Nation's Land*. Washington, D.C.: Government Printing Office.

Raiffa, Howard. 1982. *The Art and Science of Negotiations*. Cambridge, MA: Harvard University Press.

Robinson, Glen O. 1975. *The Forest Service—A Study in Public Land Management*. Baltimore: Johns Hopkins University Press.

Sax, Joseph L. 1980. *Mountains Without Handrails: Reflections on the National Parks*. Ann Arbor, MI: University of Michigan Press.

Shands, William E. 1979. *Federal Resource Lands and Their Neighbors*. Washington, D.C.: Conservation Foundation.

Shands, William E., and Robert G. Healy. 1977. *The Lands Nobody Wanted*. Washington, D.C.: Conservation Foundation.

Steen, Harold K. 1976. *The U.S. Forest Service: A History*. Seattle: University of Washington Press.

Truluck, Phillip N., ed. 1983. *Private Rights and Public Lands*. Washington, D.C.: The Heritage Foundation.

Voight, William, Jr. 1976. *Public Grazing Lands: Use and Misuse by Industry and Government*. New Brunswick, NJ: Rutgers University Press.

Wehr, Paul. 1979. *Conflict Regulation*. Boulder, CO: Westview Press.

Wolf, Peter. 1981. *Land in America: Its Value, Use and Control*. New York: Pantheon Books.

Wyant, William K. 1982. *Westward in Eden*. Berkeley, CA: University of California Press.

INDEX

ABOUT THE CONTRIBUTORS

MARION C. CLAWSON is senior fellow emeritus of Resources for the Future in Washington, D.C. He has been associated with Resources for the Future in various capacities since 1955, including directorship of the land and water studies program as well as vice president and acting president. Earlier in his distinguished career, he worked in the U.S. Department of Agriculture's Bureau of Economics and later served as director of the Bureau of Land Management in the Department of the Interior. Over a period of several decades, he has authored a number of authoritative books in the area of public lands and land-use management.

JEROME DELLI PRISCOLI is a senior policy analyst with the U.S. Army Corps of Engineers' Institute for Water Resources, Fort Belvoir, Virginia. He is an expert and innovator of practical techniques in public participation, conflict management, environmental planning, policy analysis, quality assurance, and the human aspects of building large-scale projects.

BENJAMIN C. DYSART III is past president and former chairman of the board of National Wildlife Federation, a trustee of the René Dubos Center, a senior fellow of The Conservation Foundation, member of the EPA Science Advisory Board, a former member of the U.S. Department of the Interior's Outer Continental Shelf Advisory Board and its scientific committee, a member of the National Park Service's Glacier National Park Science Council, and a professor of environmental and water resources engineering at Clemson University. He teaches graduate courses in resources planning and environmental protection, is a consultant to corporations and agencies in these areas, conducts research on linkages among components in land and water resources systems, and was general chairman of the René Dubos Center's Forum on Land Use Management.

M. BROCK EVANS is vice president for national issues with the National Audubon Society, Washington, D.C. He is now a member of the national board of directors of the Sierra Club. Prior to working with Audubon, he was director of the Sierra Club's Washington, D.C. office and was Sierra's northwest field representative in Seattle.

MARY LOU FRANZESE is a resource planner with the Potlatch Corporation in Lewiston, Idaho. She is also secretary of Federated Women in Timber, vice-president of Idaho Women in Timber, and chairman of Clearwater Industry Forest Planning Committee.

DON L. KLIMA is the chief, eastern division of project review, with the Advisory Council on Historic Preservation, Washington, D.C. The Council is responsible to the president and Congress on federal undertakings that affect historic and archeological resources, and he oversees this role in all states east of the Mississippi River, Puerto Rico, and the Virgin Islands.

DAVID CHARLES MASSELLI is an attorney-at-law engaged in private practice in Arlington, Virginia. He is Washington counsel for the Western Organization of Resource Councils, and litigates federal coal leasing and energy facilities siting in the Rocky Mountain Region on behalf of environmental and citizen groups.

FRANK J. POPPER is an associate professor in the Urban Studies Department at Rutgers University, New Brunswick, New Jersey. He is author of The Survival of the American Frontier and a board member of American Planning Association and American Land Resource Association.

ROCHELLE L. STANFIELD is a staff correspondent covering energy and environment with the National Journal, Washington, D.C. She previously covered federalism, urban affairs, housing and community development, education, and mass transportation.

JOHN T. TANACREDI is a supervisory research ecologist with the National Park Service at its Gateway National Recreation Area, Brooklyn, New York. He is a former environmental protection specialist with the U.S. Department of Transportation's 3rd Coast Guard District and Environmental Education Specialist at Gateway NRA.